FIFE AND PERTHSHIRE

INCLUDING KINROSS

FIFE AND PERTHSHIRE

INCLUDING KINROSS

ALAN HALL

PEVENSEY GUIDES

To Greta, our children
and our grandchildren

The Pevensey Press is an imprint of
David & Charles

First published 2002

Map on page 6 by Ethan Danielson

A catalogue record for this book is
available from the British Library.

ISBN 1 898630 49 6

Edited by Sue Viccars
Page layout by
Les Dominey Design Company
Printed in China by
CT Printing Ltd.
for David & Charles
Brunel House   Newton Abbot   Devon

*Page 1: Culross Palace, 1600s home of
Sir George Bruce, pioneer coal master
and salt producer*
*Pages 2–3: The massif of Ben Lawers,
Perthshire's Olympus, towers above Loch
Tay's northern shores*
*Right: Through a window of
Ravenscraig Castle, by Kirkcaldy, to the
bay below and the Firth of Forth beyond*

CONTENTS

Map of the area   6

Ancient Kingdoms, Modern Times   7

Fife – 'The Wee Kingdom'   14

1 Kincardine to Leven   16

2 Fife's East Neuk   32

3 St Andrews   40

4 Fife's Northern Shores
   & the Howe of Fife   48

5 Falkland & the Lomond Hills   55

Perthshire & Kinross   62

6 Loch Leven, Kinross & the Ochil Hills   64

7 Strathearn, Perth & Carse of Gowrie   72

8 Strathmore & the North-east Glens   83

9 Southern Grampians   90

Useful Information & Places to Visit   108

Bibliography   110

Acknowledgements   110

Index   111

FIFE and PERTHSHIRE

1. Forth Bridges – Road and Rail
2. Dunfermline – Abbey, Museum
3. Culross – Abbey, restored sixteenth century burgh
4. Anstruther – Fishing Museum
5. St Andrews – golf, R&A Museum, Cathedral, Castle, University
6. Falkland Palace
7. Tay Bridges – Road and Rail
8. Loch Leven Castle – Kinross House
9. Gleneagles – Hotel and golf
10. Drummond Castle Gardens
11. Earthquake House
12. Perth – Kinnouill Hill, parks, churches, Branklyn Gardens, museums
12a. Scone Palace, Stone of Destiny
13. Dunkeld – Cathedral, Hermitage
14. Blairgowrie – berryfields, restored jute mill
15. Meikleour hedge – world's highest
16. Meigle – Pictish Museum
17. Taymouth Castle – golf
18. Aberfeldy – Wade's Bridge, Crannog Centre
19. Pitlochry – hydro-electric, salmon ladder, theatre
20. Blair Castle
21. Queen's View
22. Glenshee Ski Centre

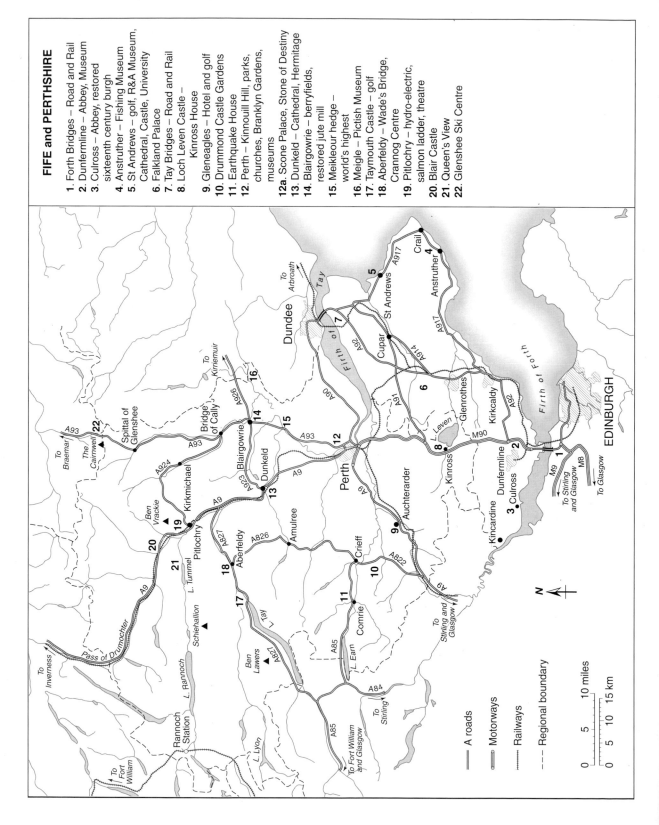

Ancient Kingdoms, Modern Times

Let me introduce Fife, Perthshire and Kinross-shire, the birthplace and heartlands of Scotland, now burdened by the 1975 designations of, 'Fife Region', containing the 'districts of Dunfermline, Kirkcaldy and North East Fife', plus 'Perth and Kinross' a 'district of Tayside Region'. These titles mask the past and dim the scenic highlights within these intriguing, ancient Kingdoms, so allow me the indulgence to present them subjectively, through written word and camera lens, simply as 'Fife, Perthshire and Kinross'.

Fife, bounded on three sides by sea, and Perthshire, land-locked save for the narrowing Firth of Tay, cradle tiny Kinross between. Collectively they present a colourful canvas of diverse, dramatic landscapes richly endowed with ancient royal burghs, palaces, cathedrals and castles. Exceptional engineering achievements, embodied by four remarkable bridges spanning the Firths of Forth and Tay, the hydro-electric schemes of

My feet they trayvel England, but
I'm deein' for the north –
My man, I heard the siller tides rin
Up the Firth o' Forth.
Violet Jacob

Forth Road Bridge: elegant and busy, connecting Fife to Edinburgh and the Lothians

Pitlochry highlights: dam, salmon ladder and floodlit power

Tummel Valley and Breadalbane and miles of Wade's military ways, excite and intrigue.

Berthed alongside Scotland's eastern coastline Fife enjoys a fine dry climate, its southern shores, described by R. L. Stevenson in *Kidnapped,* fringed by 'the firth lying like a blue floor'. Tidal waters of the Firth of Tay and the restless North Sea complete an exhilarating and varied coastline of 116 miles (186km). Backed by the Cleish and Ochil Hills, this pentagonal peninsula covers 505sq miles (1,308sq km). Blessed, or perhaps haunted, by such formidable natural barriers Fife and Fifers centuries past remained staunchly independent, prompting deleterious neighbouring Scots to mouth the somewhat unkind adage, 'It taks a lang spoon tae sup wi a Fifer'.

Kinross, by contrast, has its water within, the ethereal freshwater Loch Leven – some 8 miles (12.8km) in circumference – providing historical, religious, aquatic, geological and wildlife interest, and great fishing. Packaged within the hills of Ochil, Bishop, Benarty and Cleish it was, in the era of counties, Scotland's second smallest, a mere 81¼sq miles (210.5sq km).

Perthshire, central within Scotland, initially covered just over 2,479sq miles (6,420sq km), making it Scotland's fourth largest county. Although smaller today, it retains its appeal and nine of its burghs including Perth, described by Tennant as 'the glory of Scotland'. Between Perthshire's Highlands and the Sidlaw and Ochil Hills lie a series of fertile straths and the Carse of Gowrie, enjoying a temperate climate in which agriculture, fruit and silvi-culture, together with closely linked whisky distilling, flourish.

Geologically Fife, Kinross and south-east Perthshire emerged from the tectonic area called 'Midland Valley'. Consisting mainly of Old Red Sandstone, 350–400 million years old, it is divided by intermittent ridges of volcanic rock, manifest in Perthshire as the Sidlaw Hills, in Kinross as the Ochil and Cleish Hills, and in Fife as the Lomond Hills. Fife was also blessed, or damned, by a mix of carboniferous deposits of coal and oil-shale under calciferous sandstone, together with volcanic outcrops and sills from fusions of basalt and dolerite. Most of Perthshire, north of the Highland Boundary Fault, from upper Strathearn to upper Strathmore, contains the blue-hazed southern Grampians. Highlands of older metamorphic rocks of Dalradian and Moine assemblages, the former including quartzite, marble and schists, the latter the visually disadvantaged flagged quartzites, were sedimentary in origin, later transformed by heat, pressure and Ice Age activity into deep glens and monoliths, such as Glen Lyon and Schiehallion (the 'fairy hill' of the Caledonians).

Human history began a mere 8,000 years ago, with prehistoric European Celts probing Scotland's eastern coastline behind the retreating ice cap. Tribes such as the Venicones and Vacomagi multiplied throughout the Bronze and Iron Ages with Fife, Kinross and Perthshire at the heart of Pictish dominance during the Dark Ages. Although written evidence of their culture is absent, there remains a scatter of symbolic stones – at Balfarg (Fife), Abernethy, Fortingall, Dunfallandy and Meigle (Perthshire) – and place names prefixed 'Pit', as in Pittenweem (Place of the Caves) and Pitlochry (Stony Place). Scone later became the enthronement site for Pictish high kings.

The Roman experience was, historically, brief. Legions of Agricola, Severus and Constantine arrived between AD82 and AD306, building redoubts in Fife and forts in Perthshire and occasionally mauling the resident Picti or 'Painted Ones' as at Mons Graupius (known by name but not exact location). They were finally driven south to Hadrian's Wall around AD366 by the disenchanted locals. Centuries later the indigenous Picts, who had tenuously co-existed with Rome's legions, suffered a beating and ethnic cleansing by Kenneth mac-Alpin's Scots and a severe mauling by invading Danes, causing the 'Painted Ones' to vanish into ninth-century oblivion. For the next 200 years Scone, with its enthronement 'Stone of Destiny', along with Dunkeld, emerged as the Scots' favoured royal seat. In 1054 and 1058 Malcolm III defeated King MacBeth at Dunsinane (fictionalised by Shakespeare) to create the House of Canmore, a dynasty of fifteen monarchs, including Robert I the Bruce, whose daughter Marjorie was founding Mother of the Royal House of Stewart. Dynasties who favoured Fife, whilst recognising Scone as the traditional site of royal enthronement, from the eleventh to sixteenth centuries created a plethora of palaces, royal burghs, places of worship and Scotland's first seat of learning.

MacGregor's Leap: seen through the historic tortuous Pass of Lyon, and framed by autumn's palette

Our travels through the polymorphic 'Kingdoms' begin via the Forth or Kincardine bridges in south-west Fife and end on Highland Perthshire's northern boundaries. In between we investigate the coastline and immediate hinterland from Kincardine to Leven; probe Fife's unique East Neuk, home to those who go to the sea in ships; discover there is much more to St Andrews and its surrounds than golf; delve into the nature of the Howe of Fife and the Tay Estuary; sample the rise and fall of Falkland and scale the Hills of Lomond and Benarty; look into Loch Leven, its past and its wildlife, exploring Kinross and the Ochil Hills; scrutinise the 'Fair City' of Perth and the southern straths; pick Blairgowrie berries and keek into the north-east glens; search the solitude and legendary secrets of Grampian's glens and lochs.

GETTING THERE

Centuries ago entry was a tedious land trek via the garrisoned bridgeheads of Stirling or Perth hindered by the Ochil Hills sprawl, or alternatively by a hazardous ferryboat crossing of the Firths of Forth and/or Tay. Fortunately nineteenth- and twentieth-century engineering skills have provided four of Britain's most spectacular bridge-building triumphs, including the Victorian colossus over the Forth, and sadly one fatal disaster; 'Oh! Ill fated Bridge of the Silv'ry Tay' wrote William McGonagall. Crossing both Firths,

Aberdour: the nineteenth-century Hawkcraig Jetty welcomed the Leith 'trippers' come high or low tides

where fact and fiction mingle, are today experiences to savour and enjoy, although Dr Johnson and Mr Boswell recorded their 1773 Tay ferry 'was on the pricey side', whilst H. V. Morton *In Search of Scotland* was well satisfied with the 3/6d for his 1930s Ford four-seater.

Road access to the area's southern quadrant, fed through Edinburgh or the M8, is via the elevated Forth Road Bridge leading onto the Kinross-and-Perth-bound M90. Entry from Glasgow or the Central Belt is by the M80, the M876 or the M9 via Kincardine Bridge. From Stirling utilise the A907, the A91 or the M9–A9 for Perth and Perthshire. Northern ingress into Perthshire's Highlands is by the A84, A85 or A82 from Fort William, the A9 from Inverness or the A93 from Braemar over a realigned 'Devil's Elbow'. Perthshire and Kinross are accessed from Dundee via the A85; Fife and Kinross over the Tay Road Bridge.

Fife and Perthshire are served by National Rail services from Glasgow, Edinburgh, Dundee, Aberdeen and Inverness. Internally the 'Fife Circle' service links nineteen stations within Fife, whilst local services in Perthshire connect Perth with Gleneagles, Dunkeld, Pitlochry and Blair Atholl. And if adventure beckons, take the West Highland Line to/from remote Rannoch Station on Perthshire's north-west frontier.

Comprehensive local buses, including some school services and the postbus, plus national bus services, operate within the three counties.

International and national airports, connected by road/rail links, are Turnhouse (Edinburgh), Abbotsinch (Glasgow), Prestwick (Ayrshire) and Inch (Aberdeen).

PLACES AND PEOPLE

Discover, in Fife's medieval settlements, the benefaction of Andrew Carnegie – philanthropist, industrialist and child of Dunfermline – whilst at St Andrews, encounter reformer and rabble-rouser John Knox and golfer 'Young Tom' Morris. Lower Largo in Fife's East Neuk introduces Alexander Selkirk, exemplar for Daniel Defoe's *Robinson Crusoe*. In Kinross it was Mary, Queen 'of Scots' incarceration that highlights Loch Leven Castle, and when in Perth, recall the 1559 thunder of John Knox in St John's and the detention of fifteen-year-old James VI in the House of Ruthven (now Huntingtower). In Highland Perthshire, at Inver by Dunkeld, Neil Gow, fiddler and composer, sets our feet atapping; at Aberfeldy and Tummel Bridge General Wade's military roads and bridges stretch the legs, and in Glen Lyon Captain Robert Campbell, butcher of Glencoe, shocks the senses whilst Fortingall's claim 'Pontius Pilate was born here' beggars belief.

Devotees of the great outdoors can enjoy Fife's shoreline activities, including kite surfing and kite-ing, particularly on the West Sands at St Andrews – location for the opening sequences of the Oscar-winning *Chariots of Fire* – watersports, sailing, sea fishing, 'mucking about in boats', bird watching and so on. Coastal paths, country rambles and hill walks, developing

*Golden autumnal walks by Lochs
Faskally and Dunmore*

within Perthshire into mountain treks, abound. Cycling, mountain biking, horse riding, skiing, snowboarding, river rafting, fly fishing and falconry are among the many pursuits available, coupled with horse racing at Perth, motor racing at Fife's Knockhill Racing Circuit, for flying and gliding enthusiasts Fife Airport, Glenrothes; Scottish Gliding Centre, Levenmouth, Fife; Scone Aerodrome, Perth; and for sky-divers Strathallen. Photographers and artists enthuse about the inspirational landscapes, seascapes, skyscapes and architectural compositions. Wildlife enthusiasts delight in the many nature reserves and sites of scientific interest, particularly Loch Leven's Nature Reserve, adjoining Vane Farm Nature Centre and the Scottish Wildlife Centre at Dunkeld's Loch of the Lowes. Highland Perthshire's varied birdlife can be enjoyed in tandem with its renowned acres of colourful woodlands, including the Fortingall Yew, Europe's oldest tree.

No, I have not forgotten the Royal and Ancient game of golf, for here are quality links and parkland courses in abundance, including the holy grail of St Andrews and manicured Gleneagles.

For those who seek more sedate attractions visit North Queensferry's Deep Sea World National Aquarium, with its underwater viewing tunnel, the Scottish Fisheries Museum at Anstruther, St Andrews' Sea Life Centre and the salmon ladder at Pitlochry. Varied museums, art galleries and heritage centres interest the visitor, particularly St Andrews' British Golf Museum, Dunfermline's Andrew Carnegie Birthplace Museum, Perth's Black Watch Museum and Perth Museum and Art Gallery. Cathedrals, abbeys, castles, gardens and parks abound, including the spectacular palaces of Scone and Falkland.

The 'Kingdoms', as afficionados know and visitors will discover, have that rare virtue of endorsing that you are within these ancient lands and nowhere else, whether it be via the *sight* of Scotland's serrated skylines from Ben Lawers, autumnal golds at Dunkeld, Faskally and Killiecrankie, or the silhouetted remains of St Andrews Cathedral in evening's afterglow, or perhaps the *sound* of a train rumbling over the Forth Bridge above North Queensferry, the booming Braan beneath Rumbling Bridge, or the appreciative applause that envelopes great champions on the Old Course. Maybe it manifests itself through *smell*, the salty tang of the East Neuk, or as it did in the linoleum capital, Kirkcaldy, where the essential, but unfortunately odorous, linseed oil lingered, expressed so succinctly by Mary C. Smith in 'The Boy in the Train'.

For I ken mesel' by the queer like smell
That the next stop's Kirkcaldy.

Crail's ancient harbour, so typical of Fife's East Neuk

FIFE – THE 'WEE KINGDOM'

Yonder the shores of Fife you saw,
The gallant Firth the eye might note,
Whose islands on its bosom float...
Sir Walter Scott

FIFE, THE VERY ESSENCE OF SCOTLAND, can have no finer introduction than through its principal gateways over the Firths of Forth and Tay, spectacular passage for centuries by boat, today by bridge. Scenic delights and altars to the nineteenth- and twentieth-century bridge-builders' skills they whisk us, by road and rail, across two of Scotland's finest estuaries. Hills are small, solid and often conical, the highest – West Lomond (1,713ft/522m) and East Lomond (1,471ft/448m) – known to generations of navigators as The Paps of Fife.

The title of 'Kingdom', an imaginative misnomer much favoured by Fifers and romantics, perhaps evolved when Fife and Kinross was a Pictish sub-kingdom. Or did the royal patronage of the Houses of Canmore and Stewart, for Dunfermline, St Andrews and Falkland, raise the stakes?

Medieval Fife prospered, being rich in minerals, producing bountiful harvests from land and sea and also as Scotland's ecclesiastical and academic centre. As it did during the Industrial Revolution, thanks to its innovative mining techniques powering the manufacturing industries. Such expansion was aided by the advent of the steam train, the Forth and Tay bridges and the ingenuity and endeavour of its people, but damned by Scotland's collier serfdom, although not all coal owners practised colliery bondage. In recent times coal mines, bar one, and other traditional heavy industries, have worked their last shift, fortunately replaced with an eruption of electronics, information technology, aluminium smelting and offshoots from North Sea oil and gas.

We journey throughout the Kingdom, sectioned into five, utilising Fife's unique character and also its eccentricities; revealing as much as space allows to tempt the inquisitive adventurer to perceive, as I did, that 'A day away from Fife can be a day wasted'.

Above: The hazy Lomond Hills, known to generations of mariners as 'The Paps of Fife'
Left: Strathmiglo's remarkable classic tolbooth dominates the High Street

15

1 KINCARDINE TO LEVEN

TEN CENTURIES OF ENDEAVOUR

Our journey begins not at Kincardine but at Fife's main portal of North Queensferry. From here it is westward to Kincardine, looping inland prior to exploring the Forth's north coast and pitted hinterland.

Non-identical structures of steel and endeavour – the Forth bridges – cross the wide Forth with certainty and security. The rail bridge spans Queensferry Narrows for 1½ miles (2.4km), a Victorian colossus, now floodlit, that never ceases to excite those who travel over its rumbling rails or gaze in awe from whatever angle.

The Forth Road Bridge is an elegant arched suspension bridge of steel and concrete, bearing a two-lane twin carriageway, cycle track and footpath. I remember well the central placement of the final section, witnessed from a crowded ferry, prior to its official opening by Queen Elizabeth II in September 1964.

SOUTH-WEST FIFE

Although now in retirement North Queensferry, hunkered below the Forth bridges, appeals to many, perhaps attracted (as I) by the nostalgic love/hate relationship for the bygone days of the 'Queen's' ferry. It invites exploration on its Heritage Trail, for hereabouts can be found the hands-on aquarium Deep Sea World, a ferry jetty for seasonal trips to intriguing Inchcolm, and access to the start of Fife's scenic coastal path at Inverkeithing.

Inverkeithing (mouth of Keithing burn) is one of Scotland's oldest royal burghs, a community of traders dating back to 1164; it was also a ferry port prior to its eigtheenth–nineteenth-century expansion as a coal port, shipbreaking and paper-making centre. Weekly markets and annual fairs were

BUILT TO LAST

The Forth Bridge Railway Company took seven years to plan and build the bridge, which required 22,600 cubic ft (640 cubic m) of Aberdeen granite, 62,000 cubic ft (1,755 cubic m) of masonry, 55,000 tons of steel, 8 million rivets, and cost 57 lives. Its three cantilevers, one with a foot on Inchgarvie, carry a double rail line 150ft (46m) above the Forth by means of 340ft (104m) high towers. This vital link was opened on 4 March 1890, when the Prince of Wales symbolically drove home rivet number 8 million.

Above: Inverkeithing's fourteenth-century mercat cross, adorned by the Unicorn of Scotland, awaits 'tidings of weal and woe'

Below: Culross – seventeenth-century town house and tron (a weighing system that produced the 'Culross Chalder')

held but only the Lammas Fair remains, described in Burgh records as 'a time of fun, frolic, fit races, ale and drunken folk', and famous for its 'hat & ribbon race'.

The old town, high on the hill, has many buildings of interest; the tolbooth, 1770 tax office and prison, its Dutch 1667 town bell now in the museum in the thirteenth-century Hospitium of Greyfriars Monastery. In Bank Street stands one of the burgh's jewels, the mercat (market) cross on an octagonal shaft dated 1398, with the Unicorn of Scotland, saltire-adorned, crowned by four shields bearing the arms of King Robert III, Queen Annabella Drummond, the Duke of Rothesay and the Douglas family's Red Heart. Here public proclamations and accusations were made, 'tidings of weal and woe', for Inverkeithing persecuted 'witches' with a vigour seldom matched in Scotland. Note St Peter's fifteenth-century tower and Norman font and, opposite, turreted Fordell's Lodgings.

Westward is Rosyth (headland of arrows) naval base and dockyard, a vital anchorage during two major wars. The naval base holds an open day annually during June. Expansion and a return to the Kingdom's trading roots is anticipated with a ferry terminal planned to open in 2002, sailing to the Low Countries of Belgium and Holland.

Continuing west with the Kincardine road branch left to Limekilns and Charlestown, yesterday's working towns, today's fashionable dormitories for Dunfermline and Edinburgh, with yachts and dinghies bobbing by the pier. In the past press gangs abducted Limekilns lads for merchantmen loading from its brewery, rope works, saltpans, soap works and limekilns. It was at Limekilns' Ship Inn that Stevenson's heroes in *Kidnapped*, Balfour and Breck, stopped for food and ferry.

Charlestown (after Charles, 5th Earl of Elgin), was custom built in the 1750s, as were fourteen shoreline limekilns and new harbour, today a crumbling cameo of the days of lime, coal and wagon-ways. Leave the village north and west to Crombie in whose church and burial ground are displayed humour and graveyard symbols well worth a browse:

In this churchyard lies Eppie Coutts,
Either here or hereabouts.
But whaur it is nane can tell
Till Eppie rise and tell herself.

Culross parish and its neighbour Tulliallon were, until local government reorganisation in 1891, detached outposts of Perthshire. Its name, pronounced 'Coorus', of Gaelic origin, derives from 'cul' (behind) and 'ross' (peninsula). Birthplace of St Mungo, and religious centre, it developed into a port of importance and has, thanks to sensitive restitution in the 1930s, been brought into the twenty-first century as a vigorous citation of a sixteenth-century Fife burgh.

Coal was first dug by lay brethren, then post-Reformation this right was

leased by George Bruce, later Sir George, a pioneer coal master and salt manufacturer. His restored Culross Palace stands distinct and his mine was a seventeenth-century forerunner in drainage techniques. Another noted product, now collectable, was the Culross iron-baking girdle. Don't miss the 1626 town house and tron – an ancient weighing system that produced the 'Culross chalder', a standard measure of coal – nor Outlook Tower and the mercat cross of 1588. A stroll past Snuff Cottage to the 'hill-top' thirteenth-century abbey is most rewarding. Country and town life in the 1790s contrasted greatly, as said the Reverend Rolland of this parish: (country) 'manners are simple and virtuous, contented with their situation'; (town) 'the baneful habits of idleness and a taste for luxury and dissipation'. Adding casually, 'For twenty years there have been no murders committed, one or two child-murders excepted'.

West from Culross we pass the castles of Dunimarle and Blair, to reach the giant coal-fed power station, Britain's largest, with its 600ft (183m) chimney astride Longannet Mine on Longannet Point.

Prior to the Forth Road Bridge opening the 1936 bridge at Kincardine

Limekilns: yesterday's working town, today's fashionable dormitory, masks HMS Ark Royal *anchored at Rosyth*

Pages 20–1: Longannet, fringing the Firth of Forth – coal-fired power station alongside Scotland's last deep coal mine

Looking through the wrought-iron gates of Pittencrieff Park to the imposing statue of Dunfermline's Andrew Carnegie, a weaver's son and international philanthropist

(head of the thicket) on Forth provided the most easterly crossing between Fife and Edinburgh. Salt production was the basic industry followed by shipbuilding, and a coal-fired power station now redundant after the demolition of its 400ft (122m) twin chimneys in April 2001. We leave Fife's western outpost, with Tulliallan Castle, its neighbouring police college and Devilla Forest with its walks and picnic area, to the north, then through woodlands and marginal farms pass Comrie and Oakley to Saline, a settlement of some charm close to Fife's western marches and the Cleish Hills. Saline has survived the mining of ironstone and coal, evidence of which scars the surrounding hills, hills that offer access and ways for horses, cyclists and walkers. Visit walled 'God's Acre' with its headstones engraved 'rooms', prefixed by a number, invariably two to five, referring to the number of souls lying within; others display a plough share, the insignia of the occupant's craft, similar to Kincardine's nautical symbols.

Nearby, Knock Hill racing circuit roars around the upper slopes of tower-clad Knock Hill, north from Dunfermline on roads worn smooth by 'wannabee' Jackie Stewarts or David Coulthards. The Cleish (narrow) Hills and Blairadam Forest are somewhat featureless; Dumglow, at 1,243ft (379m) is the highest. West rise the Saline Hills, with Knock Hill and Saline Hill easily ascended from the redundant mine at Steelend. Walks, cycle tracks and horse-riding routes over these low-lying hills provide varied vistas, particularly of Loch Leven. Deep in Blairadam (clearing of Adam) dark Loch Glow nestles, providing trout fishing, run by the Civil Service Sports Association, Rosyth.

KINGS AND CLERICS

Dunfermline (hill by the winding stream) is the ancient capital of Scotland and Fife's largest town, a burgh of regality in 1125, confirmed 1588, its towers and spires basking in its past prestige and its filial benefactor. This town of a thousand years was home to the Houses of Canmore and Stewart. Eight Scottish kings, including Robert I The Bruce, several queens and princes, are buried here, and its eleventh-century royal residence was later converted to a royal palace. In the eighteenth century the hand of industry was laid on the burgh, with coal and quality linen weaving bringing growth and good fortune.

On Pittencrieff Hill King Malcolm III built his tower; the remains rest in Pittencrieff Park, known locally as the Glen. Gifted to Dunfermline by Andrew Carnegie in 1903, it covers 76 acres (31 hectares) of parkland, flower gardens and a small zoo, offering views of the Forth bridges, the steeples and towers of its abbey and the unmistakable city chambers clock tower. Grey squirrels and songbirds abound, peacocks strut; the Glen is a delight all year round, particularly in autumn with the glorious colours of acer, rowan, beech and birch.

Dunfermline Abbey, Scotland's first, wealthiest Benedictine abbey, was built 1128–1250, a cruciform facsimile of Durham Cathedral. Only the medieval nave remains, together with the thirteenth-century chapel to St Margaret, the fourteenth-century choir and the west gable above the door-

STAR-SPANGLED SCOTSMAN

Andrew Carnegie, a weaver's son, was born in 1835 at 4 Moodie Street and emigrated to America, metamorphosing into industrialist, philanthropist, author of Gospel of Wealth *and the world's richest man. Unlike Dylan Thomas, Andrew Carnegie did not forget the 'land of his father', providing 2,811 libraries, many in Scotland, in his benefactions which exceeded £70,000,000.*

Pittencrieff Park's colourful gardens and the towers of Dunfermline's fifth-to twelfth-century abbey

REBIRTH OF LOCHORE

East from Dunfermline lie the skeletons and memories of West Fife's proudest industry – coalmining. Little remains around Kelty (hard), Cowdenbeath (birchwood on coalfield), Lochgelly (white loch) and Lochore (gold loch), an open-cast mine here, a mining legend there (Jennie Lee, 1904–88, an Independent Labour Party MP at twenty-four, married Nye Bevan in 1934, fought hard and long for mining communities and in particular the Fife coalfields of her roots. Minister for Education 1967–70, she was responsible for founding the Open University, and was created a Baroness in 1970). But perhaps the most poignant monument lies in the transformation of Lochore. Once the black spot of this 'black stane' area, its long drained loch a cesspit of mining sludge, its skyline scarred by bing, belching chimney and pit head, it has since the late 1900s been transformed into Lochore Meadows Country Park: a place of clean air, thriving wildlife, watersports on Loch Ore, a golf course, rural walks and an outdoor education centre. Only the concrete superstructure of the winding gear and a mechanical replacement for the 'pit pony' of the Mary Pit remain.

Above: Lochore Meadows Country Park – this pleasing place has flowered from an industrial wasteland
Right: Mossmorran – an evening inferno emanates from North Sea gas

way. In the seventeenth-century, due to major weakness, the walls of the nave were strengthened with angular rippled buttresses.

Visitor attractions include Pittencrieff Glen, the palace and abbey, Abbot House, Carnegie Birthplace Museum, town walks and golf courses, and for further information the helpful public library. Dunfermline Athletic, whose glory days were in the 1960s under the guidance of the late, great Jock Stein, play senior league 'fitba' at East End Park.

From Lochore Meadows Country Park we pass the twenty-first century equivalent of 'pit-head clutter', Mossmorran, once a desolate plain hidden by ridge and hillock, today a belching beacon illuminating the night sky with the fire of Hades. This vast chemical complex, operated by international oil companies, processes North Sea natural gas to be piped several miles south to Braefoot Bay tanker terminal for worldwide export.

FIFE'S TRADING COAST

Aberdour (mouth of the water), a royal burgh in 1638, retains its eighteenth and nineteenth-century façade; and includes twelfth-century St Fillan's church betwixt its picturesque harbour and award-winning Silver Sands beach by the coastal path. Apparently Robert the Bruce came, after Bannockburn, to pray at St Fillan's 'Leper's Squint' ('squint'– an aperture allowing worshippers sight of the altar). Sandy rock-strewn bays, golf course and traditional harbour walls enclose the small tidal harbour, while at Hawkcraig see the skeletal 'twelve-hour' jetty of 1866 to which the Leith paddle-steamer brought trippers 'across the water'. Aberdour's railway station, built in 1890 and awarded Scotland's 'best kept station' title for eleven consecutive years, connects to the Forth Rail Bridge.

Inchcolm (St Columba's isle) lies south-west across Mortimer's Deep, named after a twelfth-century Alan de Mortimer, whose corpse was

Aberdour: harbour, sandy bay and golf course overlook the Firth of Forth

25

A WORLD FIRST

Perhaps Burntisland's greatest hour came with the world's first train–transporter ferry, the 1850 floating railway from Granton (Edinburgh). A daily programme of four passenger trains was scheduled, a 6-mile (9.2km) crossing to Burntisland, then by rail and train ferry to Dundee, a journey time of four hours. This remarkable service was the brainchild of Thomas Bouch, designer of the ill-fated Tay Bridge. His 'floating railway' was a great success, initially with the double-ended Leviathan, precursor of today's 'ro-ro' ferries.

dumped into the Forth by disgruntled monks en route to the burial isle. Although ancient, St Colm's Abbey of sanctity and sanctuary remains standing. Summer ferries sail from Aberdour.

Burntisland, for 'saut herring' the best harbour on the Forth, a salty old seaport, is on the horn of Rossend, conspicuous astride its promontory overlooked by Dunearn Hill. It is a tantalising mishmash of yesterday's solidarity and today's technology, personified by Rossend Castle (circa 1119) above the docks and Alcan Chemicals Ltd alumina plant by Aberdour Road. Kings and commoners sailed forth from Burntisland, some with loss of life and fortune, for reputedly royal gold and *The Blessing of Burntisland* lie beneath the Forth. In 1568 Burntisland received its burgh charter, the trigger that prompted its burghers to build Scotland's first post-Reformation church, St Columba's, high above the Forth. Dutch in style it stands foursquare below its gleaming golden weathercock. Cromwell visited in 1651 and to break the stalemate of siege he struck a deal. He would accept the hospitality of Rossend Castle and in return would repair the harbour and streets.

Pettycur to the east was in fact the northern terminal of the old ferry crossing from Granton, passengers for Dundee continuing by horse-drawn coaches to the Tay at Woodhaven. The first 'public' coach service in Fife, with a two-horse stagecoach, began in 1805 between Pettycur and Newport. In 1810, McNab of Cupar instigated a through service, with a four-horse coach –*The Union* – from Newhaven (Leith) to Pettycur, then via Cupar to Newport and Dundee. The tiny harbour's massive seawalls are lined with fishermen's sheds and small craft. It may have seen better days but nevertheless it's a haven of character. Two sandy beaches of Pettycur Bay, tucked in tight below terraces of caravans, gaze south to rocky Inchkeith (Island of Keith/wood), known in the sixteenth century as 'Island of Horses'. Inchkeith has provided eccentric medical research for James IV, an isolation 'hospital' for plague victims, a military base for the French and finally a lighthouse of 1803, now fully automated.

Kinghorn (blue headland of basaltic columns) profited from shipbuilding and the spinning of flax and cotton by Arkwright machines. Described as a 'sedate and sober airy town', a royal burgh was created by David I. In 1250 a royal mint was established when Alexander III instigated the 'Scottish long cross penny', his moneyers in Kinghorn being 'Wilam & Walter'. The parish church of 1894, by Nethergate to Kirk Harbour, stands on ground consecrated since Saxon times. Dr Johnson and Mr Boswell tarried awhile: 'Both dined at Kinghorn after a visit to Inchkeith'.

Leave Kinghorn north for the royal burgh of Kirkcaldy (fort of hard stronghold) – 'Cockly Cawcawdy, the Lang/Saut Toun'. The rising road, as it breeches the crest, reveals Kirkcaldy's sweep of sandy foreshore; in the words of Thomas Carlyle 'A mile of smoothest sand'.

A stroll around the old town, shore and harbour – here streets and wynds such as Sailor's Walk refer to ships, coal, glassworks, pottery and

The dramatic remains of fifteenth-century Ravenscraig Castle

linoleum – offers many clues to its trading background. Linoleum is synonymous with Kirkcaldy, although formulated in the mid-1800s by Englishman Frederick Watson. Note along the High Street the one-time home of economist Adam Smith whose *Causes of the Wealth of Nations* has been continuously in print since 1776. Architects William and Robert Adam also lived in Kirkcaldy, as did Thomas Carlyle who taught at the Burgh School.

Coal was worked in the fifteenth century, initially to fuel the salt industry and its export trade, with ninety-one vessels registered. Kirkcaldy had expanded by the nineteenth century, principally manufacturing linens, importing flax from Baltic ports and exporting cloth to England and the Low Countries. Spinning and weaving of coarse linen and canvas made Kirkcaldy a world leader in linoleum manufacture, crowned by the 1890 opening of Michael Nairn's factory, known locally as Nairn's Folly. The town hosts a fine museum, art gallery, public library and, at Dunnikier Park, an 18-hole municipal golf course and nature trail; and is home to Raith Rovers FC. There is more to Kirkcaldy than meets the eye.

From Kirkcaldy rise above Pathhead Foreshore to the headland crowned by Ravenscraig Castle and flanked by Ravenscraig Park. Entry to both is free. The castle's foundations date from 1460 and when completed was a fortress ahead of its time. It was torched by the English in 1547, and a cen-

Above: The filled-in harbour at West Wemyss. The early 1700s clock tower (right) bears a weathered panel stating 'This fabric was built by Earl David Wemyss and town for the cribbing of vice and service to the crown'

tury later Cromwell left his visiting card. In 1955 the state acquired the property and today its dramatic remains are accessed from the park and flanking beaches. The adjacent park is well laid out with a nature trail, unusual doocot, flowerbeds, bowling green, free car park, kiddies' play area and the usual facilities.

Dysart (retreat), a royal burgh in 1549, with a solid eye-catching tolbooth erected twenty years later, is adjacent to Ravenscraig Park, separated by the whammled (concealed), deep and steep, salty Hot Pot Wynd. Linen, coal, salt and nails by the million, set the manufacturing seal from the eighteenth century, exporting to the Low Countries along with beer and fish, and returning with red pantiles and pipes. Little wonder its nickname was Little Holland; it was also very popular with smugglers, prompting yet more burgh caricatures, 'Kirkcaldy for lasses braw, Pathhead for meal and maut, Dysart for coal and saut'.

By the rock-girdled harbour stands the castellated tower of St Serf's. At the tower's foot at Pan Ha' (medieval saltpans), is a small complex of tastefully restored fisherman's cottages, one, The Anchorage (1582) complete with whitewashed walls and 'crow-stepped' skews (stones forming part of the coping of the sloping part of the gables). Close by stands Bay House Inn, its lintel inscribed 'My Hoip is in the Lord 1583', while lanes named Gait and Hie Gait run from town to shore. In the 1800s the Bay Horse was Scotland's east coast ship sales centre.

From Pan Ha' green, visit the coalmining triumverate of Wemyss (coastal caves), known centuries ago as Wemyssshire, reached from Dysart by the coastal path or the A955 tourist route. The estates of Wemyss provide a rich seam of history, folklore and industry, including Scotland's first glassmaking factory known as Wemyss.

The A955 junction at Bowhouse Toll leads to the shoreline village of West Wemyss, a burgh from 1511, known as the 'haven town of Wemyss', its past prosperity powered by the 'black gold' of Lochgelly. The harbour was enlarged, and a tunnel – the 'Lochhead' – ran to Coaltown to facilitate the movement of coal. Little remains today. In 2001 the entire street and tower were renovated.

Coaltown of Wemyss is a tidy, well maintained 'model village' built to house mining families in the nineteenth century, and declared a conservation area in 1980. Its 1911 pub, The Earl David Hotel, was run on the Gothenburg system, with profits assisting the local mining community. The oldest cottages, in Barns Row, indicate that Wemyss estate workers were initially employed in agriculture rather than coalmining. In the 1890s Coaltown's population increased, due entirely to the mining boom when West Wemyss, and in particular Methil, expanded to major coal ports. Many cottages were built prior to World War I, more in 1937, all in the distinctive style of Fife's coastal settlements, with pantiled roofs, crow-stepped skews and harled white walls.

PRIDE OF PLACE

Coaltown's architectural flagship is Coronation Place (after George V1's crowning) where cottages and houses are typified by elegant arches, known as 'Tod's arches', signature of the builder in 1912, renovated by his son in 1937 and proudly displayed in floral Coronation Cottage by his grand-daughter.

Coaltown of Wemyss: Tod's Arch, Coronation Place and Coronation Cottage, dusted with winter's frost

Similar to Coaltown, but not matching in character, East Wemyss was built as a dormitory village for mine workers. Castleton was its original name, after nearby MacDuff's Castle, originally fourteenth century and now a two-towered ruin. The shoreline below MacDuff's Castle is noted for many capacious caves, several revealing markings and grafitti dating, in some cases, from Pictish times. The 'must-go' Wemyss Environmental Education Centre provides details of local wildlife, social history and industry. The path and road that brought us to Wemyss continues north-east to the working end of this extraordinary section of Fife, exiting, as we did at Kincardine, in some haste.

Buckhaven (haven of the buck) and Methil (middle wood), west of the River Leven, linked and labelled by the black hand of coal, were, in their youth, presentable, pleasing fishing and weaving villages on the western fringes of Largo Bay by Leven (flood). Buckhaven – local pronunciation 'Buckhyne' – has a hazy history concerning its early settlers; were they tenth-century Vikings or sixteenth-century shipwrecked Dutch? Whoever they were they worked hard and their fishing and weaving community prospered. In the nineteenth century coal was dug and exported, although old habits died hard. For then fishermen went to sea in summer, Buckhaven fishermen landing 25,000 haddock in one day; in the winter they dug coal, though how many tons is not recorded.

Methil, a free burgh of 1662, produced salt and was the original coal port for its neighbours, later engulfed in a tidal wave of prosperity in the early 1900s as one of Scotland's most active exporters, handling approximately 1¾ million tons per year. Football came with East Fife FC, cradle of the legendary 'Slim Jim' Baxter, in 1903, achieving national success by winning the Scottish Cup in 1938 and the League Cup three times between 1948–55. Gone are the days of Cup glory as are the quayside coal shutes, in their place the giant skeletal frames of oil rigs, today's floating 'nodding donkeys' of the North Sea.

Leven, and its river of that ilk, was in years gone by a port by the name of 'Levynsmouth', importing victuals for Falkland Palace. In 1602 the port closed to curtail an epidemic of smuggling. Leven's drive to encourage the tourist is somewhat handicapped by the power station dominating the river's mouth, although encouraged by old Leven, extensive sands, its fine golf links, Letham Glen and friendly folk.

Of the three, Methil escaped the notice of the 'rhymer', leaving us with – 'The merry lads of Buckhaven, The bonny lasses of Leven'.

Once Scotland's busiest coal port, Methil now turns its skills to oil and gas rigs

2 FIFE'S EAST NEUK

SEAFARERS, SANDY BAYS & SALT

There are Boats in the Kingdom of Fife...
R.L. Stevenson.

North-east from the sandy crescent of Largo Bay to the rocky headland of Fife Ness stretches a unique coastline of trading and fishing burghs, intermittently sprinkled between sandy bays, sea-sculptured craigs and promontories, backed by a fertile, often windswept, hinterland of high-yielding black soil. Distinct houses, traditionally harled, with crow-stepped skews and red pantile roofs, huddle around harbours crammed with the paraphernalia of those who live by the sea for the sea, prospering when the shoals came by, hungry when haddock and herring went elsewhere, cycles that ebb and flow with the centuries and man's intransigence. Bays of safe sand, fringed with challenging golf links, miles of walks and nature trails, a clutch of castles, solid churches and museums and a must for the sea angler, watersports enthusiast and those who appreciate local food. For within are some of the best 'chippies' in Britain, including Anstruther's '2001 Best Fish Restaurant in Scotland'.

'Welcome to the East Neuk of Fife' signals the links-lined A915 to Lundin Links, Lower Largo and Kirkton of Largo. Once three separate villages, today's cottages are close to becoming a holiday conglomerate. Fortunately the oldest antiquity remains, the remarkable Lundin standing stones, second millennium BC, the highest standing at 18ft (5.5m) within the Lundin ladies golf course. They stand proud beyond the first green; for closer inspection and an information sheet, please check at the club-house/starter's box.

'The saucy limmers o' Largo' (limmers – jades), said the verse. Kirkton of/Upper Largo (hillside) was recorded in the twelfth century, its impressive restored church being of that era, and later a village involved in the

Above: Lundin Links standing stones – at 18ft (6.26m) high they dwarf the lady golfers
Right: Lower Largo's nineteenth-century rail bridge and harbour relax in summer sun

FROM FACT TO FICTION

Lower Largo is a charismatic wee village, overlooking the south-facing beach, hopefully not to develop into a Robinson Crusoe theme park. For it was on the site of 99–101 Main Street that Alexander Selkirk (1676–1721) was born, marked by an appropriate castaway statue and plaque. A lad of spirit, he went to sea aged twenty-seven in the privateers' trade, only to clash with his captain, and for his actions was given shore leave on uninhabited Juan Fernandez island, 800 miles (1,287km) off Chile. Four years and four months passed before he was rescued by buccaneer Woodes Rogers. Selkirk returned to Largo in 1712 and in 1719 Daniel Defoe published Robinson Crusoe, *loosely based on Selkirk's adventures.*

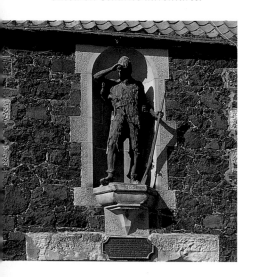

Lower Largo: on this site lived young Alexander Selkirk, Daniel Defoe's 'Robinson Crusoe'

weaving and bleaching of linen. Its celebrity was salty Andrew Wood, who defeated the English fleet in the Forth in 1498. His castle in Upper Largo has shrunk to Wood's Largo Tower and his canal, on which he was rowed to the Kirk, has now dried up.

Lower Largo was home years ago to a linseed oil mill and flax spinners, into whose tiny harbour trickles Kiel Burn beneath the redundant high four-arched rail bridge of 1856 that carried the Fifeshire Coast Express and freight (mainly fish and seed potatoes) between Glasgow, Crail and St Andrews.

PAST AND PRESENT

Largo Law, a distinctive twin-topped cone, backs Upper Largo, providing fine views, particularly over the Forth to Edinburgh. Further north at GR409073 stands Norrie's Law, site of a rich vein of Pictish silverware. Body armour and engraved personal adornments were unearthed privately and sold to silversmiths from 1819–22, who melted many pieces. What remains are suitably 'museumed'.

If time allows, walk the 5 miles (8km) or so of Largo Bay, accompanied by tumbling lapwing and swooping sand martin, to the cavern of Macduff's Cave by Kincraig Point and Earlsferry; it's an invigorating walk. Alternatively visit Colinsburgh, a 1705 custom-built village for the superfluous soldiery of Colin Lindsay, Earl of Balcarres. South nestles Kilconquhar (cell of 'Conchobar') by Kilconquhar Loch. This one time turf and peat bog had an open drain running to the sea, that is until 1624–5 when a violent wind choked the drain with sand to form today's loch, a great favourite with swans and curlers.

The Earlsferry end of Elie – they amalgamated in 1929 – is met at the coastal path signpost at Chapel Ness, the rocky point where invading Danes landed. Earlsferry has a long pedigree, a royal burgh from 1223, named after the 10-mile (16km) ferry service to North Berwick (that saw local fishermen rescue MacDuff, Earl of 'Fyfe' from the clutches of MacBeth). Cavernous MacDuff's cave by Kincraig Point was his hideout; other caves are Doo and Devil. This section of the coastal path, not to be attempted at high water, requires the assistance of a Celtic *via ferrata*. Earlsferry is understandably a magnet, not only for retirement but also for sailors and golfers, for here James Braid was born, five-times winner of the Open Championship and the only Scot in the 'Great Triumvirate' of the early 1900s.

Elie (tomb) is a friendly and relaxing family, golfing and watersports resort, enjoying its own retirement. Wide russet sands, deep harbour, coastal walks and interesting architectural mix, including the parish church, add to its attractions.

Fishing and coastal trade from Earlsferry to Crail, involving twenty-seven vessels of 1,427 tons, in addition to 226 boats herring fishing and 74 catching white fish, faded from the late 1800s, with tourism taking over as the main source of income. In the 1960s Fife's coastal railway was axed by

Beeching, an event that fired a member of staff to ignite Elie's railway station – 'no job, no station'!

St Monans or Monance, the first of the East Neuk's big three, is best approached from Elie by the coastal path. There is lots to see and savour, passing the ruined castles of Ardross and Newark, the former belonging to a pal of Robert I, the latter once owned by General Leslie. Note Newark's flues for curing game and fish, the nearby 'doocot' for fresh pigeon meat and the vaulted cellars used by eighteenth-century smugglers. This busy hard-working harbour retains its covenanting spirit, convincing all who visit that this is Fife's East Neuk, emphasised by the burgh motto *Mare Vivimus* (We Live by the Sea). The pre-Reformation parish church, by Inweary Burn, built in 1370 by David II, with its weatherworn gables, dumpy square tower, prominent octagonal steeple and eroded headstones, graces the shoreline; a kirk that muted its bell when silvery shoals came into the Forth for fear of frightening the herring away. Leaving harbour and township eastward bound, we encounter Fife's industrial past, epitomised by the wind pump, the craters of bucket pots and pan house remains of eighteenth-century salt production. From Culross to Pittenweem salt was produced, Scotland's third export after wool and fish. Trade declined when sun-dried Biscay salt and importations of English rock salt appeared. Scotland's last salt works, Prestonpans, closed in 1959.

Largo Law: the East Neuk of Fife's western guardian

BATHING IN STYLE

Lady's Tower, on Elie's East Links by Sauchar Point, allowed the lady of Ardross Castle to bathe in seclusion, her privacy ensured by her bellman having warned the folk of Elie not to disturb her lavations.

SWEAT AND SALT

Salt manufacture was a twenty-four-hours-a-day activity of steam and smoke. Seawater, fed by the wind pump into the bucket pots, and coal, from the seams of nearby Coal Farm, provided the raw materials. From the bucket pots settlings were distributed into the pans of the pan houses. Coal or pan wood furnaces reduced the water leaving salt, repeated several times prior to storage in the girnel (salt warehouse). An excise man or salt officer assessed the weight and fixed the duty.

Right: The restored eighteenth-century wind pump at St Monance, enjoying its retirement

Below: Pittenweem, headquarters of the East Neuk's fishing fleet

Within sight to the east, another mass of pantiled roofs, almost obscuring the tolbooth tower, spills down to the sea: Pittenweem (place of the cave), a thicket of lums and masts, whose harbour is home to the East Neuk's fishing fleet, a royal burgh of industry and interest. Imagine the cloud of despair that darkened the town when at least 100 local covenanting seamen died at the 1645 Battle of Kilsyth, leaving seventeen boats in the harbour crewless. A century that saw witch-hunting in Pittenweem exceed, in ferocity and time scale, even that of Inverkeithing, castigations occurring as late as 1705. Andrew Wilson of Pittenweem, a reputed smuggler, robbed a customs officer, was sentenced to death and later hanged in Edinburgh's Grassmarket. This triggered the infamous 1736 Porteous Riots, when Edinburgh's town guard fired into the belligerent but unarmed crowd of Wilson's sympathisers, killing and maiming thirty people. Pittenweem hosts, during August, the East Neuk Fish Festival.

Anstruther (the rivulet – pronounced 'Enster') & Cellardyke is the largest of East Neuks' burghs and one-time major fishing port. In 1929 the 'Anstruthers' integrated with Cellardyke and Kilrenny to meld into the mouthful of the 'United Burghs of Kilrenny, Anstruther Wester and Anstruther Easter' – Scotland's longest burgh name! The harbour by Shore Street would be buzzing with sailing ships carrying coal, linen and salt to the Baltic and Mediterranean, returning with timber, metals and wine. In 1753 a new quay was built and to pay for it an Anstruther tax of two pennies Scots was laid upon every pint of ale brewed or sold. It was noted that as the years passed the revenue fell by two-thirds! For the full story of this coast, visit the Scottish Fisheries Museum at Harbourhead, opened 1969 in buildings known as St Ayles; nearby lies the retired North Carr lightship.

Famous sons list Dr Thomas Chalmers – architect of the Free Church, his name given to Anstruther's distinctive harbour light; Capt Sir James Black – Trafalgar hero; and Professor W. Tennant who penned *Anster Fair*.

Cellardyke, once hailed as 'the cod emporium of Scotland' and unkindly as 'a dingy fisher-town', is today completely linked to Anstruther and both attract many visitors.

Kilrenny (cell of St Irenaeus) is called St Irnie by seamen who use its prominent church steeple as a navigational aid. Set back from the shoreline and main road this peaceful pint-size one-time weavers' and farm-workers' village belonged to the Beaton lairds of St Andrews. Note its 'before and after' Innergellie Doocotes by the picnic site. An eighteenth-century parish minister noted a cyclical decline in cod and haddock stocks, due to over-fishing, remarking that 'boats fishing once amounted to 500 at any one time'.

Crail (boulder rock), an 1178 royal burgh

The restored Innergellie doocot at Kilrenny, used in previous centuries to house pigeons to provide fresh meat in winter

4 miles (6.4km) north-east from Anstruther, is a unique historic, picturesque, dormitory and working town sitting high above its harbour. Three medieval streets, dwellings, harbour and castle exhibit not only a Scottish influence but also the hand of Holland. The Collegiate Church of St Mary, with its imposing gateway, spire and belfry, at the east end of Marketgate, has listened to sermons from John Knox, reformer of St Andrews and James Sharp, Archbishop of St Andrews. A sombre mercat cross and assortment of houses old and new grace Marketgate and High Street. Its tiny, tidal harbour, apparently problematic, displays in its quays vertical and horizontal masonry masterminded by Dutch women engineers. As early as the ninth century Crail was in the export business, shipping a local delicacy of smoked haddock, the Crail capon, to the Baltic and Low Countries. By the mid eighteenth century the 'silver darlings' (herring) neither visited nor spawned off the East Neuk, for reasons, postulated by Crail's Minister 'due to unfavourable weather – the encroachments of the Dutch who occasionally sweep our coasts with a fleet of nets several miles in length – or the industry of man, having thinned this species of fish'. As it was then so it is today!

Centred at the eastern extremity of the Firth of Forth, 6 miles (9.6km) from Anstruther from where boat trips on the *May Princess* are available from May to October, stands the Isle of May (isle of sea-mew). Visible, rocky, with high cliffs one mile long, this Nature Reserve teems with kittiwakes, guillemots, shags, razorbills, terns, puffins, eider duck and seals. May has experienced a colourful history. Ninth-century Danes murdered missionary St Adrian, whose coffined remains washed ashore at Anstruther. In the 1100s David I founded a priory, but 200 years on May was too much for the monks who encamped to Pittenweem. May's first lighthouse was built in 1636, a three-storey tower illuminated by a coal-guzzling brazier, with an annual appetite of 400 tons, and financed by an appropriate toll on passing ships: '4 Scots shillings per ton for English and foreign boats, 2 shillings per ton for Scottish vessels'. This light may have saved lives, but it also took two; its first keeper was drowned in heavy seas, inciting misguided folk to burn Anstruther's Eppie Lang at the stake for calling up the storm by witchcraft.

Fife Ness (headland), shrine of the east wind, Fife's most easterly point, overlooks the treacherous Carr Brigs, and is marked by North Carr Beacon: a most appropriate four-seasons terminus for our East Neuk adventure reached by car, cycle or foot, passing a disused airfield prior to far-seeing Balcomie golf links and Dane's Dike. The airfield hosted a 1914–18 spotter station, a 1939–46 naval air station – HMS *Jackdaw* – finally serving out its time as HMS *Bruce*, a boys' training camp, prompting Crail's more outgoing provosts to claim the civic title, 'Rear Admiral of the Forth'. The old runways today provide a weekend release for hundreds of 'boy racers'.

Dane's Dike, below the airfield wireless tower, witnessed Danes, retreating to Fife Ness after their defeat at the River Leven, erecting this now grassed-over stone defence whilst waiting to evacuate to their boats, and reputedly killing prisoner, King Constantine, whose body was dumped in nearby Black Cave.

WELCOME TO FIFE'S EAST NEUK

Notable visitors to Anstruther include a battle-scarred Spanish galleon that limped into Anstruther Easter for shelter and succour; it is reported they were 'hofpitably treated'. Paul Jones, born John Paul in Kirkcudbrightshire, founder of the American navy, with 'a mad, ambitious, aspiring nature', arrived in the Forth with a battle squadron in 1779 off Anstruther. They were hailed and boarded by Anstruther's pilot and crew who believed they were British. Paul Jones immediately detained the pilot, who was 'treated very uncivilly', and dispatched the crew. In 2000 the QE2, Cunard's great liner, entered the Forth and hove-to off Anstruther. Neither battered nor belligerent, full to the gunnels with golf enthusiasts up for St Andrews Millennium Open, 'Enster' and Fife welcomed them as an armada of ferries profitably plied to and fro that July week.

St Mary's in Marketgate, Crail, witnessed diverse sermons by Archbishop James Sharp and John Knox

3 ST ANDREWS

CATHEDRALS, COLLEGES, COURSES AND BRIDGES

All here are golfers – strangers, natives, all –
The sons of science, of idleness and war…
Dr Gillespie on St Andrews

The dormitory village of Kingsbarns, formerly royal grain stores, retains much of its old charm but none of its dozen 'ale-houfes'. Its obsolete castle above Cambo Sands (car park and toilet) is passed on the Crail–St Andrews coastal path, a must for coastal wildlife enthusiasts. Nearby the Victorian Cambo Gardens are open to the public from February to November.

Between the A917 and the shoreline stand Boarhills and Kenlygreen, on either side of Kenly Water, both surrounded by 'barley and tattie' farms so typical of east Fife. The countryside has witnessed many changes since the twelfth-century slaughter of the great boar, whose extracted tusks measured 'sixteen inches long and four broad', for now we have a fine road and a scenic coastal path to St Andrews Bay. The pathway in particular reveals an assortment of prominent outcrops and needles, such as Buddo Rock with its spindly crutch, Rock and Spindle, prior to Kinkell Ness and the Maiden Stone.

ST ANDREWS

North-west from Fife Ness, clustered around its spires and towers, stands sea-washed St Andrews, Scotland's ecclesiastical and academic heart. Here rested the remains of Scotland's patron saint, St Andrew, and here stands Scotland's first seat of scholarship, St Andrews University (1412). Developed by kings, clerics and academics and later sorely devastated by

Above: St Andrews cathedral's west tower stands tall in winter's sunset
Right: The West Sands provide perfect conditions for serious kite-flying

*The plagiarised sixteenth-century castle;
many of its stones now lie in the
harbour wall*

death, degeneration and the Reformation, St Andrews was fortunately restored to health, wealth and prosperity by the Royal and Ancient game of golf, its born-again university and the arrival of the steam train.

Opinions differ concerning the arrival of St Andrew's relics at the Pictish community of Kilrymont, which was, four centuries later, renamed St Andrews by Pictish King Hungus, and St Andrew declared Scotland's patron saint. The sacred remains, 'three right-hand fingers, the arm bone and three toes' were conveyed from Patras, 'west to the utmost part of the world', by the fourth-century Greek monk St Regulus (Rule). Accompanied by 'seventeen monks and three devoted nuns' the adventurous two-year journey ended in shipwreck at St Andrews Bay in October AD370. Culdee monks established a monastery, royalty encouraged pilgrimage and it became the See of the only Scottish bishopric, control of which passed from the Celtic Church to Rome. St Andrews received its first charter in 1140 from David I. Bishop Robert established the priory and St Rule's Church and by 1161 Bishop Arnold, aided by Malcolm IV, had laid the foundation of the cathedral. It was finally consecrated 157 years later by Bishop Lamberton. Edward I of England lifted lead from the cathedral and 'cast-doune' the bishop's palace (read castle) and William Wallace had Bishop Cumyn removed from office. 'Out of the toun that byschop turned fast. A wranwys Pope that tyrand micht be cald' wrote Harry the Minstrel.

The fifteenth and sixteenth centuries were to provide a period of roller-coaster rides for St Andrews. Bishop Wardlaw founded the country's first university, an event celebrated by 'indulging in the song, the dance, and the wine-cup'. By 1472 the bishopric of St Andrews was upgraded to Scotland's premier archbishopric, all of which was rudely overturned by the Reformation, a period of murders and mayhem. Patrick Hamilton was burned at the stake, on the orders of Archbishop Beaton, whose successor, his nephew Cardinal Beaton, was assassinated by John Leslie in retaliation for the torching of the martyr Wishaw. Beaton's mangled remains were dangled over the castle walls and it was said 'ane called Guthrie pisched in his mouth', described more politely by the Rev Charles Roger, 'The body – was thrown in a salted state into the dungeon'. Martyr's Monument, a sandstone monolith at the Links end of the Scores, remembers eight martyrs who perished by fire.

Reformation fever, fuelled by reformer John Knox, was followed in 1586 by a plague that claimed 4,000 lives. In the 1770s the sharp eye and sharper tongue of Dr Johnson noted 'the silence and solitude of inactive indigence and gloomy depopulation'.

Today St Andrews is a popular delight, for there is much to please and intrigue within this mix of medieval, Victorian and Edwardian. The feel of antiquity is strong, with several pageants and street fairs reliving the past such as the student inspired 'rag', the Kate Kennedy Procession in April. The town is basically composed of three roughly parallel streets, North Street with St Salvator's College, Market Street with the town house, and South Street with its decorative West Port and ruined Blackfriars Priory, which unconsciously converge on the cathedral. The castle, rebuilt in the mid-1500s, stands beyond by East Scores surrounded on two sides by sea and cliffs. Its decline, hastened by the Reformation and a bombardment, ordered by Rome, was further aggravated in the mid-1600s when the town council removed stones to strengthen the harbour.

The cathedral's necropolis is interesting, for here lie beneath wind-worn sandstone the great and not so good of St Andrews. St Rule's Tower stands high (entry by token), and provides (for those with a head for heights) a gull's-eye view of town, gown and surrounds. There are fine walks within and surrounding St Andrews: the sylvan, birdsong-gilded Lade Braes by Kinness Burn; the endless West Sands fringing the links – a favoured 'kiteing' location; or the coastal delights to Buddo Ness.

St Andrews is the recognised cradle of world golf, the R&A the ruling authority and Scotland the custodian of its traditions. It is said golf was played here in the 1200s (or was it 1400s?). Within the hallowed walls of the R&A are housed the Regalia of Golf, including a silver club, the first St Andrews trophy, donated by 'noblemen and gentlemen being admirers of the ancient and healthfull exercise of the Golf', as well as a gold medal of 1847, given by George IV, a medal that spells golf as 'Golph'. St Andrews'

Above: St Rule's Tower stands high, providing far-seeing views

Below: The Old Course 17th 'road hole', looking beyond Swilcan Bridge and the 18th to the R&A clubhouse and Martyr's Monument

ALL HERE ARE GOLFERS

Centuries past the links were managed by nature and mown by sheep. During its long infancy the great game was given its name, apparently from the old Scots verb 'to gowff' – to smite, clout or hit hard. In 1724 the St Andrews club was formed, later in 1834 to successfully petition King William IV (also Duke of St Andrews) to assign it 'Royal and Ancient'. It has hosted, from 1873 with twenty-six competitors, more Opens on its Old Course (originally twenty-two holes) than any other championship course. The Millennium Open was contested over the Old Course, the winner Tiger Woods (USA).

Guardbridge: the medieval Gair Bridge at Eden Mouth displays Archbishop Beaton's initials and coat of arms

residents have precedence when teeing-off, as the links are owned by town not club. For the complete golf story visit The British Golf Museum, behind the R&A clubhouse.

In addition to the championship Old Course the game can be enjoyed on the New Course, the Jubilee Course, the Eden Course or the easier Balgove. Also at the modernistic St Andrews Bay Golf, Hotel and Spa Complex, on the wrong end of town.

BRIDGES, FERRIES AND FLYING

Guardbridge, the original fifteenth-century Gair (or Guard) Bridge, spans the narrowing neck of Eden Mouth estuary (a nature reserve), one of the few medieval stone bridges in use today; as is Dairsie Bridge 2 miles (3.2km) west. Originally six arches, a single carriageway allowed passage of carriages only; carts and so on had limited ebb-tide passage below. The bridge provided a gathering point for St Andrews pilgrims, who in those violent times were given a guard or escort for the final miles. Now widened and pedestrianised Gair Bridge sits alongside its 1939 counterpart carrying the busy A91 to/from St Andrews. Extensive paper-mills, established 1873 on a Haig distillery site, provide local employment.

Leuchars (of rushes), overlooking Eden Mouth and St Andrews Bay, hosts two diametrically opposed features, the RAF station and the ancient church of St Athernase.

RAF Leuchars is the present HQ for 43 and 111 squadrons, and an active mountain search and rescue team. West–east runways, unseen but not unheard, lie north of the muddy Eden estuary, a far cry from its cradle days when, in 1911, it operated as a balloon spotter site, which during the 1914–18 conflict became a Royal Flying Corps aerodrome. In 1917 it was a naval spotter base, in 1920 an RAF station, from 1935 a flying school and from 1938 operated under coastal command. Jet fighters arrived in 1950 and today Leuchars is a jet fighter training station, eagerly awaiting the advent of the latest Typhoon. Its annual Battle of Britain Airshow is a September sell-out.

St Athernase, built 1183–7, dedicated 1244, is mentioned by James Boswell in 1786, 'Stopped at Leuchars – to see its amazing church with an old tower, 800 years old'. The twelfth-century chancel and vaulted apse is a superb example of Norman architecture. It has stood for 800 years, its blind arches and inserted square columns withstanding both pillaging English and destructive reformers, aptly described by H. V. Morton *In Search of Scotland* as 'this perfect poem in stone'.

Tentsmuir's (sheughy dyke) coastal flatlands are signposted Kinshaldy Beach from Leuchars. Stone and Bronze Age man lived on this exposed headland, as did a community of shipwrecked Danes. This slowly extending beach and conifer-clad hinterland attract a wide variety of plants and wildlife in addition to beach and watersports enthusiasts. Nearby Morton

Lochs and Tentsmuir Point are nature reserves favoured by a variety of migratory birds. The Forestry Commission provides a car park and picnic area and a network of forest trails for horse, cyclist and walker.

A salmon-fisher's eighteenth–nineteenth century icehouse stands by the shore (GR500267). Thick stone walls inset in banking and a sod-covered roof held crushed ice and snow, taken from frozen lochans, which then remained sealed until the fishing season began. Caught salmon, laid on boxed ice, were then repacked at the icehouse and shipped to London every second day as fresh fish. Journeys, given favourable conditions, would see the salmon in London within fifty–sixty hours.

Tayport, originally Ferry-Port-on-Craig, a ferry-port of antiquity, lies north from Leuchars and Tentsmuir by the stilted 1840s Pile Light. Initially with no jetty or pier, passengers and horses embarked from a craig (rock) hence its old name. Ferry charges in 1474 were fixed for 'Port-in-Craige at ane penny for the man, and for the horse ane penny', rising by 1790 to 2d for a man and 4d for a horse. A rail ferry, the *Robert Napier*, operated between Ferry-Port and Broughty Ferry from 1851, losing custom when the second Tay Rail Bridge became operational.

Clinging to the sloping banks of the Tay is Newport-on-Tay. This ribbon-development of Victorian dwellings displays a classic drinking fountain and welcomes at its east end the fine and straight Tay Road Bridge (1966–71), one of Europe's longest at $1\frac{1}{2}$ miles (2.4km). At its western marches stands Woodhaven, once the main ferry pier for Dundee (used by Rob Roy MacGregor in 1715) and terminal for the trans-Fife coach route. Newport was not long in getting a branch line connecting it with the Dundee Line at Wormit (snake), an event appreciated by the good folk of Newport and also by William McGonagall, affectionately dubbed 'the world's worst poet':

Leuchars: twelfth-century St Athernase, showing chancel, apse and octagonal bell tower – 'this perfect poem in stone'

> To Dundee will often resort,
> Which will be to them profit and sport,
> By bringing cheap tea, bread and jam,
> And also some of Lipton's ham.

Above: Newport's Victorian drinking fountain gazes over the Tay and the Tay Road Bridge to 'Juteopolis' (Dundee)

Left: Tayport harbour, by the Firth of Tay, with the nineteenth-century 'stilted' Pile Light beyond the pier and today's pleasure craft

Bridge over the silvery Tay

The Tay Rail Bridge opened on 1 June 1878 and closed on 28 December 1879 with the loss of seventy-five lives. This ill-fated structure of substandard components, designed by Thomas Bouch, who was knighted for his efforts, was brought to its knees by strong tides, storm winds and perhaps a speeding train, nineteen months after its grand opening. Bouch, found to have been negligent, was dismissed. Supporting column bases still protrude from the swirling Tay.

The twin-tracked Tay Rail Bridge of today, a few yards west from its predecessor, was planned two years later and completed in 1887. A little shorter, it covers 3,429yd (3,135m) and initially was operated by the North British Railway.

Below: Today's Tay Rail Bridge stretches from Wormit to Dundee

4 FIFE'S NORTHERN SHORES & THE HOWE OF FIFE

RICH HARVESTS FROM LAND AND SEA

A rippled hinterland, of the Ochil's dwindling extremities, teeters down to the Firth of Tay's southern shore: a quiet, largely unexplored, area of fertile farmland, tree-clad hills and probing valleys, seen to advantage along the highways and byways of the coastal tourist route and the 'Kingdom Route North Cycleway'. The glaciated Howe of Fife, through which runs the River Eden, presents a colourful patchwork within which the market town of Cupar and a scatter of working villages reflect the life and times of rural Fife.

West from Wormit by winding minor roads through pastoral policies is Balmerino (Balmurenach – sailors' town), a tiny village, not car-friendly. Little remains of its thirteenth-century Cistercian abbey; destroyed by Henry VIII's 'rough wooing', devastated by the Reformation and demolished when Jacobite Lord Balmerino forfeited estates and life after the 'Forty-five'. Now under the wing of the National Trust for Scotland, the abbey grounds remain blessed by venerable trees – Spanish chestnut, walnut and beech. Gauldry, a mile or so inland, was once a weaver's village. Further west the hamlets of Creich and Brunton (stream settlement), surrounded by craggy domed hills, churches, castles and hut circles, wear their past for all to see, and provide, in the case of Creich, fine views from Green and Black Craig, particularly over the Firth of Tay. Brunton's history centres mainly around the growing of flax and weaving of coarse linen.

Above: East over the Howe of Fife's fertile acres to Letham and Mount Hill
Right: Newburgh, a linen and linoleum township and one-time salmon port

Newburgh's West Port slipway into the Firth of Tay has seen busier times

Maritime transport

During the nineteenth century salmon were packed in ice and shipped from West Port quay to London's lucrative Billingsgate market, one company alone running four or five 90-ton salmon smacks. Barley from Fife farms, for brewers and distillers, was shipped to Leith and Glasgow and daily ferries sailed to Dundee.

Historical heritage

Beyond Brunton lies the considerable bulk of Norman's Law (hill of the northern men), conifer clothed, flanked by Black Craig and Ayton Hill, its rocky summit topped by an early first millennium AD fort surrounded by traces of round, stone huts. Legend states that plundering Norsemen stashed their spoils and buried their dead on the summit. Access requires permission from Denmuir Farm (GR302188). By the fertile shoreline of Flisk the shattered remains of Ballinbreich Castle stand, a mere shadow of the fourteenth-century stronghold of the Earls of Rothes, later sold to finance repairs to Leslie House.

Continuing west we reach Fife's north-west frontier 'one-street-town' of Newburgh (new stronghold), clinging to the skirts of Ormiston Hill, astride the Cupar–Perth A913, meeting first the scattered ivy-clad sand-stone remains of twelfth-century Lindores Abbey in Parkhill farm. In Lindores James I's son, murdered at Falkland, lies buried, and as with many ecclesiastical buildings Lindores was 'dang-doune' twice during the Reformation and much of what remained can be found in many a local wall and lintel. A royal burgh (1457), Newburgh stands by a stretch of Tay, known as Broad Water at flood tide and South Deep at low tide. In the 1800s Newburgh was the Tay's busiest port, supporting twenty-nine 'ale-houfes', producing linen and linoleum, trading in fish, particularly salmon, and a variety of agricultural products. In 1846 the Edinburgh and Northern Railway came to town and its one-time religious feast day is remembered in November as the Haggis Fair.

The Laing Memorial Museum houses a feast of local antiquities and should not be passed by. Legend also records that Newburgh persecuted witches. As late as 1635 parish records contain five charges of witchcraft, brought by the minister himself, against one Katherine Kay including, 'imprecating curfes against him' and concluding, 'she is of ane evill brutte and fame, and fo was her mother before her'.

Above the quarried flanks of Clatchard Craig are the remains of a Pictish fort, and near the trout waters of Lindores Loch a carved Pictish stone stands by Abdie burial ground. Now well into the low-lying Ochils leave the Den of Lindores on the twisting B936 south, fringing Pitmeddon Forest prior to dropping into Auchtermuchty (Uachdarmuc – ground of the wild boar). This town of red-pantile roofs, crow-stepped gables and high towered tolbooth, whose bell found its way from Lindores Abbey, became a royal burgh in 1517, later expanding into a handloom weaving and bleachfields centre, with a distillery and timber industry. Further agricultural ventures developed, including what is reputed to be the first deer farm in Britain. Its distinctive churchyard displays many eighteenth-century symbolic head-stones. The great MacDuff was said to have resided in Auchtermuchty; Scotland's finest accordian virtuoso, Sir Jimmy Shand, certainly did.

Collessie lies east, a pleasant mix of modern houses, weavers cottages and an imposing church, surrounded by a multitude of prehistoric sites, including Maiden fort and Collessie cairn. James V apparently favoured Collessie when he wanted to 'get away' from Falkland Palace. Continuing east the bonny adjacent dormitory villages of Monimail and Letham are met with the rounded Ochils immediately north. The tower at Monimail (the bare hill) is all that remains of an episcopal residence oft used by bishops and archbishops of St Andrews. Beyond both Fernie Castle, a sixteenth-century tower and a site with MacDuff connections is, since 1965, an opulent hotel.

THE COUNTY TOWN AND SURROUNDS

Cupar (common bogland), the heart of the Howe, lies astride the River Eden, the hub and junction of six major roads. This old county town and judiciary centre still looks the part. A fourteenth-century royal burgh chartered by Robert I, it was much visited by medieval monarchs from Alexander III to

Cupar tranquillity: the River Eden meanders through the heart of the Howe

Charles II. The prosperous market town and yarn-spinning centre's prudent merchant guild, it is said, assisted cash-strapped monarchs. North of the Eden medieval streets such as Bonnygate and Crossgate (who share the mercat cross), remain, and today many fine Georgian and Victorian buildings, including the prison of 1813 – considered too elegant to house miscreants – grace this welcoming town. Duffus Park, by Elmwood Agricultural College, a gift from a jute manufacturer of that name, includes the 1982 Douglas Bader Garden for the Disabled. The railway train came to Cupar in 1847 and fortunately this vital east-coast link still survives.

Compared with other towns in this tempestuous Kingdom, Cupar has worn well. Several black spots have been removed from sight and smell such as the old tolbooth, by Catherine Street, in whose lower floor – a stinking hell-hole – 'the accused, the profligate and the guilty' languished. To Cupar's credit, from the provost to the burghers, it was ignited and raised to the ground. No such drama removed the odorous sugar beet factory on what is now the industrial estate, just a closure. Many roads from Cupar display old-style 'finger-pointing' milestones.

Dairsie, or Osnaburgh after the style of linen brought by Flanders weavers, lies north of the Eden, its village, church and castle bearing the crown and clerical stamp of St Andrews. It's a pleasant place with a fine sylvan walk. South, under the railway and over the meandering river, lies Kemback, with woodland walks by Dura Den (a tiny gorge), a place of

Above: Cupar – the old county town's mercat cross, topped by its triumphant unicorn
Below: Kembeck's parish church

waterfalls, birds, flowers and old wives' tales. From here a minor road squirms to the crossroads and bygone posting station of Pitscottie, sixteenth-century cradle of Robert Lindsay, who wrote in Scots his anecdotal and somewhat wayward *The Historie and Chronicles of Scotland*.

North-east, the blood-stained site on wooded Magus Muir (tongue of moorland, GR456152), records, on two monuments, that Archbishop Sharp was assassinated there in 1679 while travelling from Ceres to St Andrews, and later five innocent covenanters were accused and executed. More pleasing is Ceres, a burgh of barony, venue of boisterous horse races in the June Ceres Games, reputed to celebrate the return of the Ceres volunteers who marched to Bannockburn, arriving too late to fight but in time to toast the victory. Today the village green, an arched seventeenth-century Bishop Bridge over the tinkling Ceres Burn, the Fife Folk Museum – one time tolbooth with obligatory jougs and the plea 'God bless the just' – will interest and amuse the visitor, as will Howie's great gobbet of sandstone depicting the rotund figure of the church provost. Several surrounding walks include the signposted Craighall Den, with its profusion of fine trees and wildlife.

At its north end a minor road leads west to the dramatically sited Scotstarvit Tower. This notable early seventeenth-century landmark built by Sir John Scot, although severe in appearance, was never used for offence or defence, and from its interior came an eccentric tirade against the cor-

Above: Bishop Bridge, Ceres, crossed by Archbishop Sharp prior to his assassination on Magus Muir
Below: Ceres – Howie's 'the church provost', for all to enjoy

ruption of politics entitled 'Scot of Scotstarvit's staggering state of the Scot's statesman'. Sir John, a noted topographer and poetic writer, Lord of Session and Privy Counsellor, was sacked by Cromwell; fortunately Scotstarvit did not suffer the same fate and under the wing of the NTS remains one of the country's best-preserved tower houses.

Returning from this elevated southern fringe of the Howe use the tree-lined 'backroad' route, passing the coaching halt of Craigrothie (Fell of Fort) and Chance Inn to Pitlessie. This directionally disadvantaged way passes redundant limestone works to the old weaving, spinning and cattle-fair village alongside the Eden below Cults Hill. It was here that the acclaimed David Wilkie, son of the manse, was born, and who in 1804 painted 'Pitlessie Fair', now in the National Gallery for Scotland. He became the King's Limner, Scotland, and was knighted in 1836.

Kingskettle, or 'Kettle' as it is known locally, was a place of linen, coal and lime, a convenience stop for travellers when the Pettycur–Newport coach rattled along the turnpike, later replaced by the steam engine in 1847. A mile or so north stands Ladybank, formerly 'Moss of Monegae' where in medieval times the lowland moss was worked by the monks of Lindores, who named it 'Our Lady Bog'. Monkstown, fringing Ladybank, relates to the peat cutters and the great 'moss' flanking the Eden, re-fashioned by an extensive system of drains and burns, such as the Rossie Drain. Malt and weaving featured strongly in the nineteenth century, when the town was elevated to a burgh, and became a major rail junction with the completion of the Tay Rail Bridge. Ladybank's testing golf course hosts qualifying rounds when the Open is held at St Andrews. Woodland walkers and ornithologists enthuse about Edinsmuir Forestry Commission's picnic place west from Ladybank.

Freuchie (heathery), gateway to Falkland via the A92(T) lies to the south, one time home of French masons – building Falkland Palace – disgraced courtiers and later linen weavers.

Scotstarvit Tower on Scotstarvit Ridge – perfectly preserved seventeenth-century home of Sir John Scot

Falkland's sixteenth-century royal palace – and Victorian post box

5 FALKLAND & THE LOMOND HILLS

THE RISE AND FALL OF FALKLAND

Symbolic hills and fringe habitations, within a diamond-shaped area, are ring-fenced from Falkland by the A912, A91, B919, A911, B969 and A92(T). Sparsely populated, apart from the conglomerate of Glenrothes, it contains Fife's highest ground, evidence galore of a Pictish Kingdom and a much visited home of the House of Stewart.

Falkland (crown/falcon's land), beneath the conical bulk of East Lomond, was gifted to the Earls of Fife in the twelfth century, its original castle a MacDuff stronghold, in which legend recounts murder most foul – a king's son starved to death by his uncle. Ownership changed when the Crown stepped in, the castle becoming the in-place for the 'chase', and greatly favoured by seven generations of Stewarts from James I to James VI. James II, in 1458, chartered Falkland a royal burgh; in 1500 James IV instigated the construction of the palace which James V completed in 1541. Impressive and architecturally ahead of its time, this fifteenth-century Renaissance building surrounded a central quadrangle. Northern buildings were destroyed by fire during Cromwell's tenancy; the three surviving surrounds, however, remain along with gardens, sixteenth-century royal tennis court and the palace museum with its Pictish stones.

In the late 1700s the burgh declined, in tandem with the palace, keeping its head above water by weaving coarse linen, there being 231 parish weavers. Around that time ten 'ale-houfes' flourished in Falkland, with three in nearby Freuchie, prompting the parochial observation, 'where there are temptations, some will be tempted'. What now makes this 1970 conservation area so unique is that both burgh and dwellings have largely retained their texture, thanks to the Crichton Stewart family, hereditary

RIGHT OF PASSAGE

In this narrowest of thoroughfares in Strathmiglo stood an inn, now converted into flats, with a unique open-all-hours public right of way passing through (between nos 59 and 61 today). Note the two large cement-filled bells guarding its roadside corners, strategically placed after a large charabanc removed a section of the inn's roof negotiating a passage that didn't exist.

Ballo reservoir and ruined castle on the airy Lomond ridge

keepers of Falkland Palace, and latterly The National Trust for Scotland. Seek out the 1607 Hunting Lodge Hotel, the thatched 1610 Moncrieff House and the Stag Inn of 1680 in Mill Wynd. So popular is this historic cameo, it can overflow during the season.

A few miles north-west Strathmiglo (marshy valley), a fifteenth-century burgh of two halves that grew from farming, weaving and serving Falkland Palace, straddles Miglo Burn. Surrounded by colourful productive farms, its older dwellings display distinctive cornerstones and lintels, quarried from the Lomonds, and its High Street tolbooth presents classic lines. Apparently our ancestors found this area a pleasing place to stay, for on or around the Lomonds are many cairns, tumuli and standing stones. The Pictish Strathmiglo Stone, AD700, by the churchyard, displays eroded symbols of a deer's head and a tuning fork.

THE SKIRTS OF LOMOND

An unclassified road, unsurfaced in places south of the Eden, tiptoes into a protruding finger of Kinross at Wester Balgedie, skirting the lower flanks of West Lomond and Kinross's Bishop Hill, passing several ascending pathways. The first by Bonnet Stane car park, the second, with car park, 1¼ miles (2km) south-west, the third rising on the south side of Glenalmond. Further

pathways can be accessed from the B911 leading south to Kinnesswood. At Balnethill by Easter Balgedie a fourth way zig-zags to the heights.

Kinnesswood, a neat village with Bishopshire golf course to match, clings to the southern skirts of Bishop Hill; 1746 birthplace and 1767 deathbed of Michael Bruce, 'poet of Loch Leven and composer of "Ode to the Cuckoo"'. His cottage is cared for by the Michael Bruce Trust who also hold an annual memorial service in July at Portmoak Church. Another son of Kinnesswood was Alexander Buchan (1829–1907), secretary of the Meteorological Society of Scotland, renowned for his 'cycle of cold and warm periods'. His thesis stated that the coldest days of each month occur between certain days (eg for August between 6th and 11th – correct for 2001; while December's warmest days develop between 3rd and 9th). Kinneswood provides access to the moorlands and crags of Bishop Hill.

Leslie (court pool), old name Fettykill, is now practically engulfed by the conurbation of Glenrothes. Once a prosperous flax and linen weaving town it looks today somewhat weary although revived by plastics and paper industries. Untouched by the black hand of coal it does appear to have a certain empathy with those of its scarred neighbours. Leslie House, a three-storeyed palace, described as 'the glory of Fife' by Defoe, seat of the Earls of Rothes, was in 1736, engulfed by flames. The heart of the Lomond hills, Craigmead car park, is attainable from Leslie via the ascending unclassified road to Falkland.

Glenrothes, the 'new town' astride the River Leven, with little affiliation to the Lomond Hills, save by sight, and none with the southern coastline, save by road, is today firmly anchored between Leslie and Markinch. In the 1940s post-war years, Fife had miners galore and a coalfield that was all but worked out. Yet surveys apparently revealed, in addition to an ill-founded faith in coal, a surrounding series of untapped workable seams. So in 1949 Glenrothes emerged to service the anticipated bonanza that never materialised. Indeed as far back as the late eighteenth century mining reports were prophesying there would be no Klondike by coal. To the authority's credit and with national help a phœnix of light industries, led by micro-electronics

Leslie's Bull Stone, a lump of granite grooved by chain and rope, remains on the village green. Goaded by local braves and bitten on the nose by local dogs the bull's only relief was to bury its savaged proboscis in a nearby scrape in the ground.

Above: Leslie's Bull Stone, a scarred reminder of man's intolerance

Left: Glenrothes – 'The Dream', a floral dance, one of several pleasing sculptures by local artists

Balbirnie House, now a luxury hotel, in Balbirnie Country Park

and paper, arose in this spacious town. Today it lays claim to be 'the capital of Fife' and its administrative centre. I would say go and see Glenrothes, with its displays of modern art by local artists, for there are none like it in this kingdom of ancient burghs; to ignore it would be to miss a unique piece of a fascinating and varied jigsaw.

The neighbouring burgh of Markinch (horse water-meadow), Fife's Pictish capital, goes back a long way, for at Balfarg and Balbirnie are two of the kingdom's prime prehistoric monuments, a rare single-entrance henge and a fine stone circle now re-sited in Balbirnie Country Park. Ancient lands desecrated by the mining of coal have been restored with the estates much extended, classical centrepiece Balbirnie House, now a hotel with a golf course, bridal paths, woodland walks and nature trails. South-east of Markinch stands Balgonie Castle with its fifteenth-century tower, highly rated by experts, together with church and Session House, both incorporating medieval features. Subsequently Markinch became an important player in the weaving of linen, followed by paper, eighteenth-century coal and Haig & Co, whisky blenders.

THE PAPS OF FIFE

The Lomond circle is squared by returning to Falkland via the A92(T) to New Inn, a major coaching stop now dismantled, and the A912 in preparation for a ramble over Fife's most distinctive hills. The volcanic Lomond Hills, umbilically linked with neighbouring Kinross's Bishop Hill, although small in stature, present well known profiles throughout and far beyond the Kingdom. They display a high land semi-circle, their western and northern faces steep and craggy, cradling several reservoirs south of the central ridge, populated with a clutch of waterfowl including swans, widgeon, grebe, redshank and sandpipers. The hills provide miles of stimulating hikes and far-seeing vistas, plus two prehistoric hillforts. One, Maiden Castle (GR222068) is an isolated mound with a visible rampart by its eastern portal; the other occupies the summit of East Lomond, its encircling ramparts crowned by a Bronze Age cairn. Taken singly the three hills, with their resident roe deer, fox, finch, cushat and grouse, provide interesting walks. Traversed collectively they present an invigorating day out, revealing great lumps of the Cairngorms and the Grampians, and over the sparkling Firth of Forth views of the metropolis of Edinburgh.

East Lomond's summit presents a somewhat formidable challenge. The bark however is worse than the bite, for there are at least five routes of varying lengths and steepness on offer. From Falkland there are two routes, a short sharp ascent, initially through conifers, on its north side, or an angled way through Bluebrae Plantation. Another ascends from the A912, via Purin Den to the picnic area and viewpoint by the 'towers' astride Purin Hill. The picnic area is also attainable from Glenrothes' Pitcairn car park, or alternatively from Easter Glasslie or Craigmead car park.

West Lomond at 1,713ft (522m) is Fife's highest. The most popular ascent is from the Forestry Commission's Craigmead car park.

East Lomond's coned dome beyond Harperlees reservoir cycleway presents upland solitude

Other ascents commence from Strathmiglo through Drumdreel woods between the cliffs of Graigen Gaw and conifer-clad Arraty Craigs. A no-nonsense path (from GR185082) takes the shortest and sharpest route to the stone-scattered summit, whilst another, a varied pleasing line, ascends alongside Glen Burn to Glen Vale, through Covenanter's Glen with its white sandstone cliffs (Strathmiglo lintels), by Bonnet Rock, prior to emerging on the plateau leading east to Harperlees reservoir or north to West Lomond's summit. Another option is the pathway, south of Glenalmond hospital, that strikes north, below the west face of Bishop Hill, to Glen Burn there to join the path ascending Glen Vale.

Bishop Hill – an undulating grass- and heather-clad plateau, steep sided above Loch Leven – provides extensive views of Kinross and Perthshire over Loch Leven to the Ochils. Although not marked on OS maps its 1,509ft (460m) northern summit can be reached from Glen Vale. A more direct approach ascends east from Balnethil via a zig-zag to the southern heights. Rock climbers, no doubt, take these routes when searching for the dolerite pinnacle known as 'Carlin (witch) Maggie', a rare feature in these parts.

The west scarp of Bishop Hill, from Glenalmond, displays winter's grip

PERTHSHIRE & KINROSS

These are Scotland's heartlands, for here Lowlands and Highlands forgather, within whose bounds diverse sensations, scale and scenery are rarely equalled, amply illustrated by a sea-level entry to Perth, with the mouth of the Tay, and an exit over a modernised 'Devil's Elbow' at The Cairnwell, Britain's highest 'A' road. Perth was the capital, Scone the site of royal enthronement, Abernethy and Dunkeld the spiritual centres; the pedigree is irrefutable. Heavy industry did not develop, as in Fife, allowing the productive hand of farming and its related cultures to produce a prosperity that sits lightly on this charismatic canvas. No matter what your interests, Perthshire and Kinross will provide a cornucopia for all.

The area's extensive acres limit an in-depth view. It is therefore my intention, with the written word and an inquisitive lens, to present an objective and subjective portrayal of as many highlights as possible, hoping to kindle your curiosity to delve deeper. I have divided the area into four divergent sections, looking first into the extraordinary wildlife and reflective waters of Loch Leven prior to a foray into the neglected Ochils, then spilling out, in the footsteps of Picts and Romans, onto the flat-lands of Abernethy to investigate the broad acres of Strathearn, the Fair City of Perth, and its granary and larder the Carse of Gowrie. Which in turn introduces Strathmore, cotton mills – neither dark nor satanic – raspberries by the basket, Pictish symbolism, the world's highest hedge and finally downhill on the pistes of Glenshee. We end with a proliferation of Perthshire's Grampians, highland probity and perfection, through which flows the River Tay, Scotland's longest and finest salmon river.

Loch Tay, west from Kenmore to Meall Greigh and Ben Lawers

6 LOCH LEVEN, KINROSS & THE OCHIL HILLS

Predominantly agricultural Kinross-shire, Scotland's second smallest county (prior to annexation to Perthshire in 1929), occupies a fertile basin encircled by an assortment of low-lying hills, described in the 1890s as this 'sleepy hollow of Scotland' with 'Loch Leven, the jewel in its heart'. To the east West Lomond and Bishop Hill delay dawn's light, south stands whale-backed Benarty together with the rippled Cleish Hills, whilst north and west the bulkier Ochils provide a formidable barrier.

Loch Leven, an elemental freshwater loch, is without doubt the magnet that attracts. Without it few would stop to admire and enjoy what was Kinross-shire, save for a cursory glance to Benarty and Bishop Hill as they hurry along the M90. There are interests for all, historical, religious, aquatic, geological, botanical and particularly ornithological, Loch Leven being a National Nature Reserve, with adjoining Vane Farm the first Nature Centre in Britain, a Site of Special Scientific Interest and an RSPB reserve. Some 8 miles (12.8km) in circumference and the source of Fife's River Leven, Loch Leven's two significant islands, St Serfs – site of a previous priory and much favoured by nesting birds – and the smaller Castle Island, by Kinross promontory, invite exploration.

A migratory destination and nesting site for wildfowl, waders and ducks, regarded as one of Britain's largest, this naturally nutritious loch also attracts mallard, widgeon, shelduck, shoveller and black-headed gulls. Four centuries ago the loch was reduced in size, by enlarging its outlet into the

Above: Loch Leven – evening fishers go forth after the renowned pink trout, below Benarty Hill
Left: Loch Leven looking to Kinross with its cashmere mills, and the sunlit Cleish Hills

65

QUEEN MARY'S MISFORTUNE

Mary Queen of Scots was imprisoned within Loch Leven Castle's grey tower in 1567 and from where, after many miserable months, she escaped, aided by Willie Douglas, the castle's boatman. Today only the keep and outer wall are recognisable. Regular boat-trips, summer only, ferry to and from the jetty by Kinross House cemetery.

River Leven, apparently to increase Kinross House frontage. The warm waters and prolific underwater vegetation provide an ideal habitat for greatly prized, pink-fleshed, silver-scaled trout; its scenic attractions are metres ahead of William McGonagall's iambics:

Beautiful Loch Leven, near by Kinross,
For a good day's fishing the angler is seldom at a loss,
For the loch it abounds with pike and trout,
Which can be had for the catching without any doubt.

KINROSS-SHIRE

Kinross (head of the promontory), is a 1540 burgh and the old county town of Kinross-shire, its overall image a little dented since local government removed its county and the busy M90 deprived its narrow, tortuous streets of through traffic. The tolbooth of the early 1600s remains, although converted into shops and dwellings, as does the old town cross and its 'jougs'. Between town and shoreline stands Kinross House, 'the most beautiful and regular piece of architecture in all Scotland,' wrote Defoe. Sir William Bruce, architect and political go-between, acquired Kinross estate in the 1680s and created Kinross House, originally for the Duke of York, later

Kinross House: the Bruce family mausoleum overlooking Loch Leven

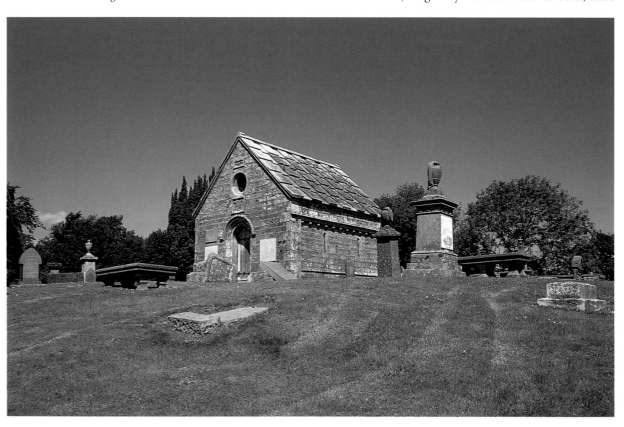

Milnthort: by the A911 stands the remains of the stronghold of the Balfours of Burleigh

James VII. Much taken with both house and surrounds, he kept it for himself. A small burial ground overlooking the loch to Loch Leven Castle displays the mausoleum of the Bruce family. Although surrounded by the well-farmed Plain of Kinross, the town retains its traditional weaving industries of cotton and linen, in addition to spinning the world's finest cashmere at Todd & Duncan. During the 1939–45 conflict the RAF manned a small aerodrome on the outskirts, later used by a local gliding club, renamed the Scottish Gliding Centre, and now sited, as the skies and droning tow-planes indicate, at Levenmouth; an altogether more suitable site, utilising the thermals of Benarty and Bishop Hills.

North of Kinross, the sister settlement of Milnathort, a one-time weavers' town, stands astride six roads. Not large, but a devil to negotiate in poor visibility, it had at one time a disproportionate number of pubs and licensed hotels, no doubt to service those who came from far and wide to trade at its busy livestock mart. East from Milnathort the now roofless sixteenth-century stronghold of the Balfours of Burleigh leans over the A911. Note its rounded tower onto which a square attic room was added in 1582. Much older are the two prominent standing stones of Orwell (GR149043), on a site of Bronze Age cists and burials, prior to Wester Balgedie, whose Toll Tavern recalls the droving days.

67

RUMBLING BRIDGE

Rumbling Bridge, an eccentric double bridge over the River Devon gorge, gets its name not from an engineering defect but from the water-rattled rocks in the fissure below. Way-marked walks confirm the rocky commotion.

Rumbling Bridge: tiny spring flowers colour the fissured trunk of a giant beech on the bonny banks of the River Devon

HILLFOOTS

As there is no urgency to reach Strathearn let us journey westward, to Yetts o' Muckart or Crook o' Devon and Rumbling Bridge, a confusing triangle on both sides of the irregular regional boundary, in search of the winding grassy pass of Glen Devon and Glen Eagles that squirms north through the Ochils to Auchterader and Strathearn. But first a word about the two gateways into Glen Devon, known as 'hillfoots'. Crook o' Devon (elbow of the Black River), has been shaken twice, but never stirred, the first time in the 1600s when it held a well-publicised witches' trial, resulting in death by fire for several of the coven and the warlock. A large stone in the dyke of Peat Gate lane is said to mark the execution site. The second trauma occurred after the Kincardine bridge was opened in the mid 1930s, allowing an ever-increasing flood of traffic, on what is today the A977(T), to shatter the Crook's rural tranquillity.

South of Clackmannanshire's 'Bermuda Triangle' the Yetts o' Muckhart (gates of swineherds) is the hamlet Pool o' Muckhart, said to have been promoted, prior to local reorganisation, as the county town of pastoral 'Muckhartshire'. The Yetts, once a toll on the drove road through Glen Devon, from 1812–13 charged for '13,219 Sheep at 5d/score and 836 Cattle at 1s/score'. To the north rise the Ochils, allowing passage from Yetts o' Muckhart via the A823 through Glen Devon and Glen Eagles to Strathearn's Auchterader and the writing tree-lined switchback of the B934 to Dunning.

THE OCHILS

The Ochil Hills (uchil – high), are predominantly Old Red Sandstone. Eroded lavas and igneous intrusions rise within the geological 'Midland Valley' of Perthshire, north of the carboniferous limestone and coal seams of Fife, presenting a coniferous and grass green blanket of rolling hills, split asunder by steep-sided valleys, probing cleuchs and busy burns. Within our boundaries, east of the north–south rift of Glen Devon and Glen Eagles (not the raptor but a contortion of the Gaelic eglise – church), are the lower north-eastern and eastern Ochils. Compared with those north of the Highland Line these hills, of repetitive tussock-clad domes interspersed with secluded grass-clad, reservoir-filled glens, may be considered dull. Large areas, despite the shallow dry soils, provide in abundance a wealth of moorland fauna and flora ranging from buzzard and kestrel to the tumbling peewit and plaintive curlew on ridge and fell, to chattering finches, woodpeckers, ring ouzels and shy herons by wooded cleuchs and tumbling streams. A colourful floral carpet will greet the walker in spring and summer, for trails are accessible on the valley floor, and to such tops as Corb Law 1,476ft (450m) above Corb Glen, reached from the Forestry

Commission's car park by the B934 Dunning road. Other FC parks/picnic sites can be found by Burnt Hill, Innerdouny Hill and Warroch Hill.

The principal route to Strathearn is via the A823 north from the Yetts, passing the roadside Castlehill Reservoir, the only visible one of five passed along the way. Glendevon, with its pleasing watering hole and youth hostel, gateway to Borland Glen, marks a change of direction as river and road (sadly lacking in parking spots) veer west beyond Glendevon Castle, its fifteenth-century core home to the 8th Earl of Douglas (a Red Douglas – descendants of the illegitimate son of the 1st Earl of Douglas) who was stabbed to death, during dinner at Stirling, by King James II. At Glenhead the River Devon continues west, to the reservoirs of Lower and Upper Glendevon, nipped tight between the steep sides of Bald Hill and Wether Hill. These hills are, and have been since medieval times, home to the ubiquitous sheep, and should be respected at the lambing time of April–May, by observing the Country Code and keeping dogs under complete control.

From Glenhead continue north through Glen Eagles, passing the modernised old toll house, leaving the Ochil's long, less dominant, variegated northern slopes that spill into the enormity of Strathearn. Journeys north through the lower eastern Ochils are by comparison much easier and equally scenic, courtesy of the sweeping M9, the B996 through well-watered Glen Farg and the A912 to Bridge of Earn and Perth.

Pages 70–1: Glen Eagles – the ever-widening mouth of the glaciated glen, north to Gleneagles Hotel, Strathearn and the rising Highlands beyond Crieff

Below: Ochil Hills – Castlehill reservoir north to Ben Thrush – summer tranquillity in morning's soft light

7 STRATHEARN, PERTH & CARSE OF GOWRIE

An M90 entry, north over the Ochils from Milnathort, sweeps eagerly between the rounded domes of Pottiehill and Balmanno Hill onto the flood plain of the broad strath of the River Earn. This easy access provides a panoramic view of what lies ahead, passing, to the east, the archetypal tower of Balmanno Castle, a fine introduction into this county of castles, prior to journeying east to Abernethy; alternatively reached through the picturesque confines of Glen Farg. Contrary to popular belief it has no connection with the 'Abernethy' biscuit created by one John Abernethy. Abernethy, centre of a Pictish Kingdom and Bishopric, is derived from Abhair Neachtain (the work of Nectan) a fifth-century Pictish ruler and founder of its church. A mercat cross and memorial grace the town's small square.

MARTYRS AND INNOVATORS

West by the meandering River Earn, barely 33ft (10m) above sea level, stands Bridge of Earn (water/Ireland), overlooked to the north by Moncrieffe Hill (hill with the trees), an ancient gateway to Perth and the Highlands, and visited throughout the centuries by intruding Romans, English kings and Protector and finally by Mar's destructive Jacobites. An earlier eighteenth-century village on the Earn welcomed steamer excur-

A TOWER OF THE TIMES

At the centre of Abernethy can be found a unique Irish Celtic round tower, one of only two in Scotland, made up of sixty-four courses of hewn stone, 74ft (22.5m) high and thought to be eleventh century or earlier. It served as a watch tower, a rather cramped refuge for the Culdee and Augustinian monastery, a place of penance and allegedly a prison. At its base, by the gateway of St Brides, lies a Pictish symbol stone displaying flowing lines and a mason's hammer. Access to the tower is by courtesy of the 'key keeper' at the tearoom opposite.

Left: Kinnoull Hill and its conspicuous folly overlooks the meandering River Tay, between the Carse of Gowrie and Strathearn, to Fife's northern shores

The broad fertile acres of Strathearn, seen from Moncreiffe Hill, enclosed by the Highland Line and the Ochils

sions from Dundee and Perth. Today's village has its 1830s Rennie bridge and Pitkeathly Wells carbonated spring water, marketed from 1910 by Messrs Schweppes, perhaps prompting Rev Thomson to pen: '…its people combine some of the best characteristics of both Highlander and Lowlander, the natural courtesy, imaginativeness and good physique of the one, the shrewdness, integrity and diligence of the other.'

South lies Kintillo, possibly Scotland's oldest 'clachen', beyond which teeters seventeenth-century Ecclesiamagirdle House, pronounced 'Exmagriddle'. Flat on the valley floor is Forgandenny, a hamlet of stately homes, Strathallen School, local characters and strange events. For between 1660–3 thirteen souls were condemned to a witch's death, and by Forgandenny Church, the Covenanter's Stone of 1678 commemorates the fatal torment of Andrew Brodie. On a less sanguine note it was at Forgandenny that Preston Watson experimented with powered flight between Rossie House and the Earn from 1903–10. His glider, launched from a suitable tree, was later fitted with an engine, which after several years and ten propellers achieved powered flight.

Leaving martyrs and innovators behind we pass the 'model village' of Forteviot, west of which stood the CAD850 Pictish palace of Kenneth mac-Alpin, who united Pict and Scot, prior to Dunning (Iron Age fort). This forms the lynchpin of six converging roads, highlighted by St Serfs

MAN'S INTOLERANCE

Women, accused of witchcraft, suffered death by burning in Kincladie Wood. One such was Maggie Wall in 1657, although no record of her name or conviction can be traced. A cairn, replaced cross (a symbol of repentance for an innocent victim?) and lettering mysteriously renewed to this day, records her death by the B8062.

Dunning: today's memorial thorn tree, in Thorn Tree Square, remembers the 1716 holocaust

with its Norman tower and Anglo-Saxon windows. Throughout the centuries Dunning has felt the force of man's intolerance as displayed at Dun Knock Iron Age fort, Agricola's marching camp and in Church Wynd, Straw Cottage, survivor of Mar's 1716 holocaust, a disaster commemorated by a thorn tree that stood for 220 years; the present incumbent graces Thorn Tree Square. Centrally placed in fertile Strathearn, Dunning hosted Perthshire's 'Fee-ing' Market (for hiring farm servants), which would account for the preponderance of hotels and ale-houses.

Above: Gleneagles Hotel – the southern façade of this incomparable luxury hotel

Below: Drummond Castle Gardens are beyond compare and not to be missed

The ever-present Ochils overlook Auchterader (high water), known, understandably, as 'The Lang Toon'. The Rev Duncan recorded in the eighteenth century it was 'dry and good in summer, rather moist and damp in winter', as is most of Strathearn. Surrounding the town are traces of Roman encampments, a hunting palace of King Malcolm III and ruined St Mungo's Chapel, spoken of as a 'Popish place'. Once a royal burgh, torched by Jacobites, it mysteriously lost those privileges. Was it due to the Calvinist 'Auchterader Creed' of 1717 or the later 1838 'Auchterader test case' between Kirk and Parliament that exploded into 'The Disruption'? It has however regained its royal burgh status.

This town of linen weavers and later woollens is today, in spite of military and pastoral turmoil, a bright dormitory tourist town geared to its neighbouring Gleneagles Hotel and golf courses. The London Midland and Scottish Railway, prior to and during World War I, built the hotel, which was utilised as a military hospital and miners' rehabilitation home in World War II, an enterprise that has expanded into a unique hotel and sports complex of style and luxury due in no small measure to its scenic sur-

rounds. Gleneagles, a personal favourite with its championship Kings, Queens and Monarchs courses, is not the only golfing magnet in Strathearn, for there are varied courses at Auchterader, Comrie, Crieff and Crieff Hydro, Dunning, Foulford Inn, Muthill, St Fillan's, and Whitemoss at Aberuthven.

Beneath its stylish bridge the River Earn flows by Comrie's old church and community centre

Saturated with golf and cashmere, Drummond Castle Gardens by Muthill south of Crieff provides a delightful change. A castle that was, as were many in Perthshire, forfeited after the 'Forty-five', knocked about a bit by Cromwell, venue of kings and queens and site of a family murder. Pride of place however must go to the formal garden, one of Europe's finest.

MOVERS AND SHAKERS

Comrie (confluence), Strathearn's western portal, stands at the confluence of Glens Artney and Lednock. There is more to this small town, with its 'Rennie' bridge over the Earn – considered Perthshire's most graceful – than its Museum of Scottish Tartans with 1,300 patterns, or the obelisk on Dunmore Hill to Henry Dundas, 1st Viscount Melville, nicknamed 'King Harry the Ninth'. For Comrie, sitting by the Highland Fault Line, is Scotland's earthquake centre, highlighted in 1839 when seismologists recorded sixty tremors, in tandem with 'a loud report and sulphurous smells'. The British Geological Survey's instruments can be seen in Earthquake House.

RUTHVEN RAID

Historically colourful, of dour demeanour, the fifteenth-century stronghold of Huntingtower (Ruthven Castle) provided the backdrop for the 1582 conspiracy known as the Ruthven Raid. Protestant lairds, gathered by the Ruthven's 1st Earl of Gowrie, detained the adolescent James VI against his will. The King either escaped or was freed and the 'Gowrie Conspirators' were punished in the fashion of the times; Earl Gowrie was put to death in 1584 and in 1600 the new Earl and his brother were also executed. To erase the name of Ruthven forever, Ruthven Castle became 'Huntingtower'.

Above: Ruthven Castle – 'Huntingtower' – where a king was detained and a lover leapt

Right: Time stands still by the Murray Fountain in Crieff's central James Square

Five miles (8km) east, through the fertile strath, stands Strathearn's 'capital' Crieff. The second largest township in Perthshire, with the largest 'hydro', it spills down to the sinuous River Earn. Named Drummond, after its laird, it also was put to the Jacobite torch in 1716. After the flames the original name of Crieff (Crubha Cnoc – hill of trees) was restored. Its eighteenth-century tryst (October cattle sale) attracted droves of cattle from the Highlands and Islands and hordes of buyers from the Lowlands and England, and witnessed 30,000 black Highland cattle changing hands. Although profiting greatly from the tryst, Crieff disliked the drunken riots that accompanied the sales, which were eventually transferred to Falkirk in the 1770s. After its 'wild west' years Crieff returned to normality, helped by its industry, education, and Victorian advent of the railway, spas, tourism and retirement.

Central James Square hosts town hall, Murray Fountain, the burgh cross and jougs. Parks, monuments and memorials surround the town providing varied walks, including Macrosty Park and the Murray mausoleum at Monzievard.

East from Crieff ridged and rolling farmlands rise from the twisting Earn to ripple north to the Grampian foothills beyond Glen Almond; historic lands that hold relics of Agricola's Roman road running via Findogask to the impressive Agricolan and Severen camp at Ardoch by Braco. Glen Almond, fashioned by temporary advances of Highland ice, exchanges its highland guise, at the southern portal of the Sma' Glen, for an agrarian aspect and a new name – Logiealmond (hollow of river), prior to joining the Tay at Perth. Glenalmond or Trinity College, a public school of note, stands by the River Almond; further east the dour stones of Methven do not. Almondbank, wrapped around the writhing Almond, one time a bleaching and dyeing centre and naval stores, leads to picturesque Pitcairngreen (place of green and cairn), complete with 'green'. Having saved the best for last we arrive at Huntingtower Castle by the bleaching village of Ruthvenfield, angled between the A9(T), A85 and Perth's burgh boundaries.

Now restored and administered by Historic Scotland, its romantic side was verified by no less an authority than the eighteenth-century nomadic chronicler Thomas Pennant. Seemingly the original structure consisted of two towers some 10ft (3m) apart, a chasm leapt by the 1st Earl's daughter as she hurriedly left her love nest to avoid detection.

THE FAIR CITY

Perth, referred to as 'Scotland's Ancient Capital' and 'The Fair City' is without doubt ancient and fair, but neither a capital nor a city. This in no way detracts from its appeal for it is a grand and stylish town of dignified terraces, museums and theatre, extensive colourful parks with bosky riverside walks and many distinctive places of worship. Tennant's words 'the glory of Scotland' still apply today.

DR ANDERSON'S OLD WATERWORKS

Note this neo-classical rotunda at Tay Street with a triumphal column (built in 1832) housing its advanced plumbing and mechanics. Power came from a steam pump, the column acting as a chimney. It served Perth until 1965 when it was internally gutted and later became the Ferguson Gallery. The rotunda and its column remain, with its Latin motto, Aquam Igne et Aqua Haurio – Water I draw by fire and water.

Perth (pronounced 'Pairth'), meaning 'thicket' in Pictish Gaelic, and its suburbs have a thriving population in excess of 42,000. Standing south of the Highland Line, alongside, and today astride, the tidal River Tay, it rightly claims the appellation 'Gateway to the Highlands'. It is not to be passed by, this portal with access to the sea, said by Pennant to have sprung from a Roman fort at the confluence of the Almond and the Tay. Rebuilt down-river by William the Lion, it was later named 'St John's Toun'; a name since adopted by the town's premier football team – St Johnstone. The name 'Perth' came centuries later, during which time it was besieged seven times and periodically washed not only by the floodwaters of the Tay, but also by waves of military and personal violence.

Edward I removed Scone's Stone of Destiny and in 1396 Perth's North Inch witnessed a refereed clan battle, in which thirty MacPhersons and thirty Macintoshes slugged it out, allegedly to settle the chieftainship of Clan Chattan. Umpired by Robert III, on what is now Charlotte Street, watched by the great and the good, few survived. In 1437 James I was assassinated by Sir Robert Graham in the royal lodgings at Blackfriars, and a century or so later surges of sectarian violence were triggered when John Knox from within central St John's Kirk, on Thursday 11 May 1559, fired the canon of Reformation that was to ricochet throughout Scotland. In 1651 Charles II felt the covenanters' wrath, whilst Cromwell transferred the prime masonry from Greyfriars to build his, now defunct, South Inch citadel. Throughout Perth, street names reflect the past life and times of its citizens: Blackfriars, Greyfriars, Meal Vennel, Flesh Vennel, Guard Vennel and Curfew Row, in which stands the designated dwelling of Scott's heroine the 'Fair Maid of Perth'.

Perth, a royal burgh in 1125, was a royal residence from medieval times and from the thirteenth century an expanding centre of trade and commerce, producing quality linen, cotton, leather and paper goods, linseed oil and milled grains for malt, beer and oatmeal. A museum and art gallery stands at the Perth Bridge end of Charlotte Street by North Inch, an impressive exterior of three colonnades matching the fine art and local history within. Impressive also is The Black Watch Regimental Museum in Balhousie Castle on North Inch.

Bridge-builders, centuries past, were plagued by the systematic spates of the River Tay, prompting the regular use of ferries. Today's bridges range from the aesthetically pleasing arched Perth Bridge upstream from the simple lines of Queen's Bridge, the functional Tay Railway Bridge and the 1978 double carriageways of Friarton Bridge. Smeaton's nine-arched Perth

Bridge of 1771 (widened 1869) replaced Mylne's bridge of 1616, demolished in the destructive 1621 flood, when the good burghers of Perth were 'wet in their beds'. Note at the bridge's ends completion tokens and flood marks. Queen's Bridge, a 1960 replacement for Victoria Bridge, is neat, unlike the railway bridge of 1863, with its twelve iron girder spans and ten stone arches.

North and South Inches (watermeadows) are today colourful, pleasant recreational areas. North Inch, the larger, provides football, golf, cricket and indoor sports; South Inch bowls, putting and kiddies' play areas. The latter is overlooked by the Georgian houses, and St Leonard's in the Fields with its prominent crown steeple, of Marshall Place. The harbour of Perth, a vital cog in town and county trade, enabled goods, prior to decent road and rail links, to be transported rapidly, including Tay and Earn salmon.

Encircled by prime agricultural and horticultural land, producing top-quality grain, vegetables, fruit and stock, it is not surprising that Perth enjoys the accolade of being one of Britain's centres for distillers, brewers, maltsters, horticulturists and one of the world's leading livestock marts, fronted by the renowned Perth bull sales, held annually in February from 1864, today bi-annually in February and October.

Flanking Perth are three hills with fine viewpoints: Moncreiffe Hill, with access to enjoy its flora and fauna and the magic of the 360° panorama; another, Kinnoull Hill (head of rock), clothed with mixed woodland, rising from the Tay's south banks above the colour-full Branklyn Gardens, now a public park gifted by distiller Lord Dewar. With adjoining Binns Hill they

Smeaton's fine nine-arched Perth Bridge of 1771, spanning the Tay, from the art gallery and museum

STONE OF DESTINY

The 336lb (153kg) Stone of Destiny, the keystone of enthronement and coronation of rulers of Dalriada, Scotland, England and Britain, remained in Westminster until removed, on 25 December 1950, by student Nationalists, to be returned several months later via Arbroath Abbey to London. With Devolution the Stone of Scone came to lie in state within Edinburgh Castle. In January 2001 'Robbie the born-again Pict' presented a plea for its removal from Edinburgh to an undecided venue (probably Scone or Perth Museum), although he and many others believe the nomadic rock is not the original Stone of Destiny, which reputedly lies hidden in Perthshire soil.

Early nineteenth-century Scone Palace proudly displays its towers and turrets

are the western extremity of the Sidlaw Hills, providing far-seeing vistas via a web of ascending paths. Summit paths above precipitous cliffs overlooking the silver ribbon of the Tay, although not overtly exposed, require care in the vicinity of a towered folly, allegedly built by Lord Grey of Kinfauns, after viewing castles above the Rhine.

SCONE

Scone (ancient mound – pronounced Scoon) and New Scone are a mile or so north-east from the burgh boundaries. Scone, an ancient and revered site, was a Pictish capital and site of the twelfth-century Augustine abbey where Scotland's monarchs were enthroned (crowning only occurring after the 1200s). Although England's Edward I purloined the stone and a Celtic bell for Westminster, Scone continued to crown Scottish royalty until 1651. The abbey was by then in decline, having suffered sectarian persecution by the fanatical fire of Reformation.

The Policies of the Abbey were granted to a relation of the Murrays of Atholl, who became the Earls of Mansfield, present owners of the 1802–5 Gothic Scone Palace, built on or near the site of the ancient abbey. Deposed Old Scone residents, mainly weavers, had to migrate to New Scone, to make way for terraced lawns, pines and peacocks, described in the 1951 Statistical Account as 'And thither the people of Old Scone trekked'. Scone Palace, open from Easter to late October, fully deserves a few hours of visitor's time.

David Douglas, the nineteenth-century botanist and plant hunter who gave his name to the Douglas fir, was born in Scone. West lies Perth racecourse, and north at Newlands is Perth Aerodrome, built in 1936, a civil, at times military, establishment, and later a school of aviation and aeronautical engineering.

GOWRIE'S CARSE

Carse of Gowrie (carse – reclaimed alluvial land; gowrie – an old section of Perthshire), alluvial lands of high fertility, Perth's garden and larder with hardly a square yard uncultivated, lying betwixt the north shore of the Firth of Tay and the Sidlaws' Braes of Gowrie, was described by Lithgow as 'an earthly Paradise'. Lands that also bear a liberal scatter of Pictish relics, medieval castles and mansion houses, including the 'added-to' Castle Huntly.

Villages are few, but as with the countryside, of delightful aspect, such as Errol with its 'Cathedral of the Carse', the one-time tiny Port Allen, once the 'harbour of the Carse' where windjammers, in the late 1800s, loaded Carse potatoes for London, and Rait (fort), a time-warp hamlet on the Braes of Gowrie. Inchcoonan Brick Works north of Errol, a company dating from 1855, with distinctive beehive kilns, produced the red bricks seen in many Carse buildings. Reed beds on the Tay estuary (SSSI) are harvested every sixth year for cottage thatch.

8 STRATHMORE & THE NORTH-EAST GLENS

The 'Great Strath' and its Perthshire neighbour, the Grampian watershed, are a topographical contrast, yet there exists an interdependent harmony. Indeed much of Strathmore's sands and gravels came from Grampian glaciations via the Ericht valley. North from Perth and Scone, we initially follow the great sweeps of the Tay and later Rivers Isla and Ericht through Strathmore, bordered by a pleasing prospect of tidy farmlands, tended woodlands and an assortment of hummocks. Confined by the wavy profile of the Sidlaw Hills south-east and north-west by the Highland Line backed by the ascending contours of Glenshee and Strathardle, the whole is a sparse scatter of villages and townships, ever decreasing as the Highlands approach. This bountiful strath has seen many pass through: weavers, spinners and bleachfield workers, military road builders, drovers with their black cattle, berry-pickers of Blairgowrie and seekers of the snows of Glenshee.

Top: To Glenshee Ski Centre – a summer's view up Gleann Beag via the A93 beyond Creag Dhearg to The Cairnwell

Above: Strathmore – bountiful lands to the Highland Line, between Coupar Angus and Meigle

83

THE BELL MILL

In its eighteenth-century heyday Scotland's first and largest producer of cotton the Bell Mill, powered by the Tay, its huge chimney surrounded by East, Mid and West Mills, employed around 1,200 workers. When the cotton bubble finally burst mill and village became silent, until 1995, when this empty shell of the Industrial Revolution was restored with the conversion of East and Mid Mill into flats and houses.

LINEN, WOOL AND COTTON

Stanley (after Earl Derby's daughter – Amelia Stanley), by the Tay, was built in the 1780s by G. Dempster, advised by the Arkwrights, financed by the Duke of Atholl and Perth entrepreneurs, as a custom-built cotton mill and village between Campsie Linn – site of the retreat of fictional 'Catherine Glover Scott's Fair Maid of Perth' – and Thistle Brig. Stanley provides extensive scenic pleasures, by nipping up the nearest hill, as noted by D. Cumming in his *Guide to Auchtergaven* – the grandeurs of the Grampians, the Ochils, the four conical 'Laws' of Fifeshire and the 'Fair City' of Perth.

Bankfoot, by the A9(T), originally a weaving village, is now agricultural, although its 'MacBeth Experience' visitor centre may classify it as a tourist venue. If time allows Bankfoot provides a good hike through Glen Garr to Rumbling Bridge over the River Braan. North-east of Bankfoot, over the Muir of Thorn at the junction of the Perth–Dunkeld railway and the B9099, is Inchtuthil Fort close by the hamlet of Murthly. Strategically sited on an elbow of the Tay this extensive first-century Roman fort housed ten cohorts of 480 men. It was apparently abandoned and methodically dismantled soon after completion providing surprising details of the fort's layout and structure, including an 'operating theatre' and some 850,000 iron nails.

Caputh's attractions were the now replaced Victoria Bridge, with its three spans of latticed girders from the fateful Tay Rail Bridge, and its handsome church overlooking the village. The church replaced its sixteenth-century predecessor on condition that no burials are in the church or the yard surrounding, a place of justice centuries gone, where whipping post and 'jougs' stood. The addition of a steeple transformed the building, according to Rev Routledge Bell, into 'one of the loveliest places of worship in the county'. Surrounded by fine stands of mixed woodlands the village and its environs are a haven for at least 300 species of wildflowers and many birds. East of Caputh, we meet the one-time weaving village of Spittalfield (hostel), which was built in the aftermath of the 'Forty-Five' as a model geometric village around its 'Muckle Hoose' (the linen marking and weighing house, now under the wing of the National Trust for Scotland).

Beyond is Meikleour, whose time-worn village cross, the fifteenth-century one replaced in 1698, was the fourth on the Brechin-to-Dunkeld pilgrim's route, from where, until the 1850s, royal proclamations were read. Also displayed are its tron for weighing wool, a whipping post with jougs and the staging and hiring station. A fifteen-minute stroll from Carsie Road via a woodland path takes us to 'Cleaven (divided) Dyke' a Roman, or perhaps Neolithic, earth wall flanked by two gullies.

Above left: Stanley's Bell Mill, Scotland's first and largest Arkwright cotton mill
Left: A Pictish carved headstone – with a Greek cross and animal heads, on the reverse a single horseman

A Pictish story

East to Perthshire's boundary, on Strathmore's fertile floor that flanks the Isla, there stand the settlements of Coupar Angus, so named to distinguish it from Cupar Fife, as it once stood in the county of Angus, and Meigle, an interesting Pictish centre whose Historic Scotland Museum displays at least twenty-five symbolic stones and slabs with many tales to tell: classic survivors of the ancient inhabitants of Scotland, symbolic carvings include Daniel in the lion's den, a camel and a swimming elephant, in addition to many enthralling sweeps of Pictish symbolism. Alyth, a small burgh of red sandstone with a hint of Holland, one-time centre for cloth manufacture, is a pleasing place, with historical items of interest and a folk museum.

Our interests lie west on the A926 to Blairgowrie (clearing of Gabran), 'Blair' to locals, with its bi-lingual street names, along with adjoining Rattray (fort settlement), alongside the River Ericht. Prior to 1777, when the Auld Brig o' Blair was thrown across, no bridge connected the two towns, passage being by weir for wheeled traffic, and ferry by Cobble Pool to Rattray's Boat Brae for pedestrians; the whole known as 'Ferry Town'. Blairgowrie and Rattray, separate parishes each with its own castle – Blair's with its green ghost, church and hint of reformation – expanded from 'mean and thatched houses' in the late 1700s to a flourishing burgh; due mainly to the Muckle Mill of 1798 for spinning flax. Others followed and in the late 1800s sixteen flax and jute mills flourished. By the 1960s the boom had ended, with silent skeletons lining the Ericht; Rattray's restored Keathbank Mill provides an interesting insight into those bygone days. Blairgowrie also has a lively spring and autumn livestock mart.

The Meikleour Hedge

Meikleour is famed for the unique Meikleour Hedge that attracts many visitors, confirmed in the Guinness Book of Records *as 'the tallest hedge in the world'. Planted in 1746 to replace an unfinished wall, (unfinished as the stonemasons had fought and died at Culloden), it was pruned for fifty years, then from 1800 'let go' to reach today's staggering proportions of 1,968ft (600m) long and 110ft (30m) high. In order to prevent it enveloping the A93 The Hedge is given a short back and sides every decade, in past years by a forester in the tree-tops with a hand flail, today in a mechanical hoist with modern pruning devices.*

Left: Cargill's Leap over the River Ericht, named after a bid to avoid capture by Claverhouse's dragoons (see page 86)

Blairgowrie's berries

Scotland cultivates in excess of 7,000 acres of commercial raspberries annually, of which some 6,000 acres are grown in Perthshire and Angus, an enterprise, originating at the end of the nineteenth century, inspired by J. M. Hodge, solicitor of Blairgowrie. With Blairgowrie as its centre, the big red Raspberry of Blairgowrie, an appropriate match for its red sandstone buildings, provides the bulk of Britain's jams. So extensive are the 'berries' they require an influx of seasonal pickers from the industrial Central Belt.

A prominent son of Rattray was the Covenanter Donald Cargill, whose strong 'Cameronian' opinions led him to lose his ministry from Barony Church, Glasgow, later to be charged with treason. Pursued throughout Perthshire to the Borders by Claverhouse's Dragoons, he escaped by leaping the Ericht at signposted Keith Falls (Cargill's Leap). Eventual capture led to execution by beheading at Edinburgh's mercat cross in 1681.

Varied walks, through and around the twin towns, reveal a fascinating insight into their life and times. A 'Walk by the River' seeks out the old mills, a trail to 'The Loon Braes & Old Rattray' visits the old bed of the Tay, the 'Bleachfields' of yesteryear and today's 'Berry fields'; 'Walk to the Darroch' is a floral delight and a trek to 'Knockie' (Hill of the Stones) reveals much of Perthshire's scenery. Golfers can enjoy Blairgowrie's renowned championship course, Rosemount.

HIGHLAND BOUND

North with the winding A93 out of Strathmore to the tweed-weaving visitor-friendly Bridge of Cally the landscape signals that Highlands are ahead as we skirt the dramatic Ericht gorge making for the confluence of the River Ardle and Blackwater, a gateway introducing the active and adventurous to two fine glens, left for Strathardle with the A924 and right for Glenshee.

Strathardle is gentle and sedate from Bridge of Cally to the memorial junction by Kirkmichael, a grey village in dreich winter days, that improves with summer sun, for it has a fine bridge, way-marked walks and a colourful history. Dalrunzion Moor yielded prehistoric remains, including hut circles and standing stones; pottery, bronze pins and a weaving comb are displayed in Perth Museum. Standing stones, in Gaelic 'clach sleuchda' (stones of worship) can be seen by Stylemouth, and at Balvarran cup holes appear in the Baron's Stone. In Covenanting times, Strathardle witnessed six armies cutting great swathes through the glen and in 1653 Cromwell's men insensitively skirmished in Kirkmichael's churchyard. In 1715 the clans mustered in 'Bannerfield' for 'Mar's Jacobites' prior to marching via Moulin to the unevenly drawn Battle of Sheriffmuir. When clan, pastoral and political conflict subsided commerce came to Kirkmichael; cattle markets, first at Balnakeilly by the Siller Burn and later at Market Moor. The village was established as a major 'stance'– an overnight watering hole for the drovers and their black Highland charges. They came from north and north-east, rambling via the Lairig Ghru and Gleann Fearnach (of the Alder Field), or over by Cairnwell to Spittal of Glenshee to Kirkmichael and onward via Ballinluig and Dunkeld, or Blairgowrie and Dunkeld by Amulree, to the great 'trysts' at Crieff or Falkirk.

Wooded Enochdhu (dark moor), with its signposted hillwalks, continues with the A924 through the narrowing valley to Straloch and enclosed Glen Breachan. Beyond, betwixt snow poles over desolate moorland, the road travels south-west to Pitlochry, marked by a roadside memorial, 'In memory of John Souter (shoemaker) who perished in a snowstorm 1892'. Should longer walks be your forte, then follow the rewarding Cateran Way, a 60-mile (96km) journey from Blairgowrie through Strathardle by Kirkmichael to Enochdhu and onward to Spittal of Glenshee, branching south-east via Glen Shee and Glen Isla to Alyth and west to finish at Bridge of Cally.

North from Bridge of Cally, the A93 ascends 1,542ft (470m) following Blackwater, Shee Water and Allt a' Ghlinne Bhig (burn of little glen) to Glenshee Ski Centre at Cairnwell Pass; initially through Glen Shee (of the fairy-hill) to Spittal of Glenshee, one-time hospice and shanty for storm-bound travellers. Dominated by the dark mass of Ben Gulabin (hill of the curlew), half-hidden and mountain-fenced by a close-knit mass

Above left: Central Alyth Burn, serene below the distant 'arches' of St Moluag's
Left: Blairgowrie's raspberry fields above Loch Rae annually provide the 'big red berries' to fill Britain's jampots
Right: Kirkmichael burial ground, 1653 site of an irreverent incursion by Cromwell

WADE'S WAYS

On the slopes of Cairnwell, west of the Devil's Elbow and the A93, lies the track of an eighteenth-century military road, the 1748–53 Coupar Angus to Fort George via Glenshee and Braemar, built by General Wade's one-time lieutenant and successor, the bon viveur Major Caulfeild. It was one of a network (exceeding 1,000 miles/1,600km) of military roads and bridges that opened up the Highlands, frequently met in the Grampians. Working parties, labouring from June to November, and consisting of a captain, two subalterns, two sergeants, two corporals, a drummer and 100 men using shovels, picks, crowbars, sledge-hammers, barrows, screw-jacks and gunpowder, built roads, 16ft (4.9m) wide with stone snow markers, as straight as possible, with zig-zags only over mountainous terrain. A remarkable feat.

of melancholy domes, it exists today as the service station for the ski-slopes above. Three glens radiate north-west and north from the foot of the great doorstop of Ben Gulabin. Our route, often thought of as Glen Shee, is in fact Gleann Beag (small glen), into which the reset A93 ascends. Climbing north to Cairnwell Pass the road overlooks the pre-1960s notorious hairpin known as the Devil's Elbow, remnants of which are visible prior to the summit, at 2,199ft (670m) Britain's highest trunk route. My memory recalls a 1948 descent of 1 in 8 at the wheel of a Sunbeam Talbot, via the Devil's Elbow, to Spittal of Glenshee, when I saw little of the hills but a lot of the tarmac.

Glenshee Ski Centre lies at Cairnwell Pass, the region's principal portal to Aberdeenshire. Gaze at the tundra-topped peaks of the Cairngorms (humped mountains) from this far flung, scree-flecked finger of Perthshire, Britain's largest ski area. It all began, in the late 1940s, with a powered ski-tow, which in the late 1950s was developed with ski-tows and lifts and runs of varied grades on The Cairnwell, Meall Odhar (dun-coloured hill) and Glas Maol (bare green hill). Today's 'Cairnwell Chairlift' takes summer and winter visitors to The Cairnwell. For mountaineers and Munro-baggers a clutch of 3,000 'footers' invite inspection from The Cairnwell.

Stunted in heather, and scarcely a tree;
And black-looking cairns of stones, as mon-
uments to show,
Where people have been found that were lost
in the snow.
William McGonagall

It can't be that bad – surely!

Right: From the retired Devil's Elbow: a brief
January glimpse of Creag Leacach

9 SOUTHERN GRAMPIANS

The southern Grampians deplore cramped monotony, as displayed in the district's highest hills of Ben Lawers (hill of the hoof – 3,983ft/1,214m), Schiehallion (fairy hill of the Caledonians – 3,553ft/1,083m) and its classic glaciated glens, such as Glen Lyon and those cradling Lochs Rannoch, Tummel, Tay and Earn. Trees abound today, an oasis that in the past was a sylvan desert, noted by Dr Johnson's sharp pen in 1773: '…a tree in Scotland is as rare as a horse in Venice'. Sir Duncan Campbell clothed naked Drummond Hill above Kenmore. A clarion call taken up by the 'Planting Dukes of Atholl', instigators of eighteenth-century forestation establishing growth on Craig a' Barns (rocky cliff) above Dunkeld, by scattering cones by cannon. Today the area includes Britain's highest and Europe's oldest, trees.

Access throughout is generally good, following in the footsteps of Wade's military roads, for: 'If you had seen these roads before they were made, You would hold up your hands and bless General Wade'. The Perth–Inverness A9(T) passes by or links with many places of interest; however, due to recurring switches from dual carriageway to two lanes, it requires total concentration.

Imagine your right hand, with fingers and thumb outstretched held palm up, and with a little imagination, you have an eagle's-eye view of the lay of the land. The heel of your thumb to its tip represents Strath Tay, Strath Tummel and Glen Garry, the pinky as Loch Earn, the third finger as Loch Tay, second finger Glen Lyon and the index finger Lochs Tummel and Rannoch, thus enabling places to be presented in an orderly, logical and informative fashion as they radiate north and west from Dunkeld.

DUNKELD TO DRUMOCHTER

If Perth is the Gateway to the Highlands, then Dunkeld (fort of the Celts) is the Entrance. A religious settlement, founded by St Columba's monks, it grew in importance when Kenneth I (mac-Alpin) made it his ninth-century capital, advanced further by Alexander I and the consecration of its cathedral. Conflict however was never far away, for during the Reformation and following Killiecrankie, cathedral and town were ransacked.

General Wade considered Dunkeld a prime site to span the Tay. However initial contacts between the heritor, the Duke of Atholl, and Wade

Schiehallion: truly the 'Fairy Hill of the Caledonians', captured from Wade's Road above Aberfeldy over Appin of Dull

ruffled the feathers of both, causing the General to bridge the Tay at Aberfeldy. It fell to a later Duke to finance a bridge, a pleasing seven-arched, grey sandstone one built in 1809 by Telford, with tollgate and house at its south end. A toll bridge was as frustrating as no bridge so, led by Robertson, known as 'Dunonnachie', the disgruntled populace removed the gates and launched them into the Tay. In 1879 tolls ceased. Town water came from Loch Ordie (of the round hill), fresh and constant; unfortunately Dunkeld's sanitation was not so well served up to the 1930s, older houses using men only 'public lavatories' sited in the back closes. Women had to empty their 'guzunders' through a hole in the lavatory wall.

Dunkeld has musical history; abbot and monks practised and taught within the cathedral and in the eighteenth-century Neil Gow, composer and fiddler of nearby Inver, entranced the land with his music, as did his descendants. 'Modern' Dunkeld's Cathedral Street is mainly early eighteenth century, tastefully restored by the National Trust for Scotland, overlooked by the ethereal cathedral gazing over shaded lawns to the Tay. Neighbouring Birnam (warrior steading) and Little Dunkeld lie over the Tay, and yes, Birnam Hill featured in Shakespeare's *Macbeth*, although Birnam's glories lie by the restless River Braan (wheelbarrow) flowing through a tree garden, the Hermitage/Ossian's Hall: a must in the red and golds of autumn, along with woodland walks by the rivers Tay and Braan and such grandstands as King's Seat below Polney Crag or King's Seat on Birnam Hill. Towering over the Hermitage is Britain's tallest tree, a Douglas fir standing 212ft (64.6m) in 1994, but higher now.

The Hermitage: autumn's colours flank the turbulent River Braan

East from Dunkeld on the Blairgowrie road the vistas are soft and bosky, studded by the sparkling 'five glacial lochs', including Lowes, a nature reserve, Butterstone and Clunie (pasture), magnets for ornithologists and anglers. North from the hamlet of Butterstone stands craggy Benachally (colourful hill), with obligatory cairn and 1800s monument. Small and sombre in appearance it is a grandstand for full-circle sightings of Lowland straths and Highland hills, including Ben Lawers, Schiehallion, Beinn Dearg (red hill), the Atholl Hills to Glas Moal, and south the Sidlaws, Fife's Lomond Hills and the Ochils of Kinross. With good light it is possible to glimpse the profile of Edinburgh's Arthur's Seat, some 51 miles (81.5km) distant.

North-west alongside the Tay to Pitlochry is a squeeze between the conifer-clad Craig a' Barns and Craigvinean. Strath Tay, with its scatter of prehistoric and Pictish culture much in evidence, widens, its horseshoe riverbanks prone to flooding by Dowally (cut-off). The tiny church of St Anne's, its neck height 'jougs' transfixed in the wall, peeps shyly over its burial ground to the latticed iron and five stone piers of

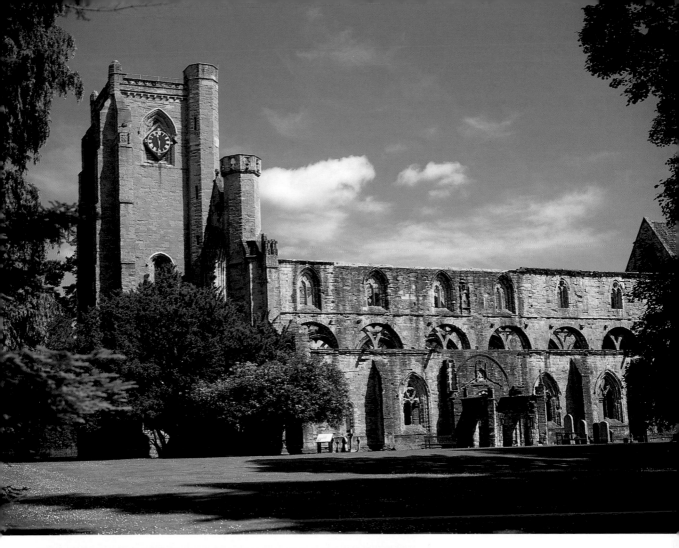

Above: A superb setting for Dunkeld's thirteenth- to fifteenth-century cathedral, sadly defaced during the Reformation and the aftermath of the Battle of Killiecrankie (see page 95)

Left: Winter ice and a sinking sun enhance the appeal of glacial Butterstone Loch

93

Above: Seventeenth-century Moulin Hotel, forever warm and welcoming

Right: Above Pitlochry rises Ben y Vrackie – in winter's cloak looking over the highland folds west to Rannoch

Below: Pitlochry – sculptured 'Lady with the Pram of Flowers', by the entrance to Atholl Palace

Dalguise Rail Bridge. Overlooking the picturesque confluence of Tay and Tummel are Ballinluig (town of the wet hollow) and Logierait (hollow of the round fort). The latter, one-time 'seat of justice', is the older, its Victorian rail bridge now pedestrianised and used by local traffic. Of the prison that once held 600 prisoners from the Battle of Prestonpans, little remains save the iron gates, now in Blair Castle, and the 'foonds' and floor of both jail and courthouse at the rear of Logierait Hotel. 'Mort-safes' remind us that body-snatchers Burke and Hare probed into Strathtay. Today's horror is the fatal A9(T) ill-designed approach from Ballinluig.

Pitlochry (stony place), a burgh in 1947, lays claim to be Scotland's favourite holiday resort, a township of sculptures and flowers, epitomised by the 'Lady with the Pram of Flowers', by Morag Cumming. Pitlochry blossomed after an inspection by Queen Victoria in 1844 and the coming of the steam train in 1863. In addition to Loch Faskally, the diminutive Loch Dunmore (with its 'table-leg' footbridge) and Tummel Linn, there are Pitlochry's Festival Theatre (new premises 1981) and Blair Atholl Distillery. Over the River Tummel and under the A9(T), the fascinating Pictish Dunfallandy Stone displays animals, angels and crosses. Of all Pitlochry's attractions the Hydroelectric Visitor Centre, dam and salmon ladder interest most. The power station draws its water from Loch Faskally, which provides a salmon hatchery and public fishing. Port-na-Craig House by the dam is the control and nerve centre for Scottish Hydroelectric; accept their invitation 'Visit the Visitor Centre, see the salmon ladder and hear The Salmon Story'. For walkers there is Pitlochry's October Autumn Gold Walking Festival.

Edradour Distillery by the musical Edradour Burn, east of Pitlochry, is a diminutive distillery producing but twelve casks a week of Edradour single malt, distilled in commercially small copper stills, confirming the old distillers adage – 'the smaller the still the finer the taste'.

Moulin (small bare summit) was a settlement of significance in 1276, the Moulin kirk being the first in Atholl, that declined when Wade's road, some distance west, was built. Moulin is a gem, with fine dwellings and an interesting kirk on the site of its predecessor. In the burial ground note the twelfth-century Crusader's grave, now occupied by 'W.M.D. aged 73 in 1808', a 'joug' on the old ash and the unique 1749 Dutch bell cast by Peter Bakker of Rotterdam that, by intention or accident, has the '4' in the date lying on its side. The seventeenth-century Moulin Hotel – an old coaching inn – standing stones, Casteil Dubh (Black Castle) and Moulin Burn add appeal. A hub for many way-marked walks and excursions, including Moulin's grandstand Ben y Vrackie (speckled hill) named after its summit scatter of coloured schists, quartzite and mica.

By car or foot it's but a short distance to Garry Bridge – free car park and Killiecrankie Pass (pass of the wood of aspen trees). High above the tree-packed Pass of Killiecrankie and the surging Garry the bridge provides unparalleled views into the pass and also passage to the historic 'Road to

the Isles'. Views north through the cleft of Killiecrankie over the trees and Meall Mòr (big lump) to the stern of Carn Liath are stunning in autumn. Below the bridge a web of fine walks, rich in wildlife, are available through this historic Site of Special Scientific Interest.

Blair Atholl (flat clearing of), known as 'Blair-in-Atholl', is a curious mix of estate village and tourist centre, the prime attraction being archetypal Blair Castle, ancient home of the Dukes of Atholl. The Castle originated from Comyn's thirteenth-century tower, enlarged twice and pounded by Cromwell it was supposedly 'broken' by government forces only to arise again to withstand a Jacobite battering. The castle and the Atholl Country Collection are open to the public. By Bridge of Tilt to the Atholl Hills are two fine, yet differing, glens of Tilt (fertile) and Fender (turf), the former long, narrow and heading to Deeside. The latter, a saucer of tranquillity, contains little Loch Moraig (Morag's loch) reputedly a fine trout loch, headed by the dominant Carn Liath (hill of grey stones) and Beinn a' Ghlo (hooded hill).

West from Blair Atholl to the Falls of Bruar (crushing falls) introduces Clan Donnachaidh Centre (Robertson) Museum, now unfortunately closed until further notice, and a modern shopping complex, the House of Bruar. The falls, reached from the museum, tumble through spectacular

Jacobite rebellion

The Battle of Killiecrankie (1689) was the apex of the first Jacobite uprising, when 2,500 Highlanders led by 'Bonnie Dundee' – John Graham of Claverhouse – locked horns with King William's army of 4,500 under General Hugh Mackay. Positioned on the heights in the narrow pass, Claverhouse with musket and broadsword finally brushed aside Mackay's broken men. John Graham fell dying, as did thousands, remembered at the Claverhouse Stone. Walk by the Garry, see the Soldier's Leap and visit the National Trust Visitor Centre. The battle site however is in private property.

95

DEER AND STALKING

Hinds and stags live apart, coming together for the rutting (mating) season in September and October, a time of bellowing and posturing. Antlers, symbol of the 'Monarch of the Glen', are cast in March and calves are born late May and June. During stalking access may be restricted, so inquire from the appropriate estate office or tourist office.

Above: Struan – three bridges in one astride the River Garry, the lower one road, the upper two rail

Right: A reflective River Garry eases through an autumnal Killiecrankie Pass below Garry Bridge, a mile or so south of the battle site

eroded rock, dramatically illustrated by the gouged arch below the lower bridge, prompting Robert Burns to pen, 'The Humble Petition of the Bruar Water', requesting the 4th Duke of Atholl to: '…shade my banks wi' towering trees, And bonnie spreading bushes'.

Bruar Lodge lies 7 miles (11.2km) up Glen Bruar, below Beinn Dearg, where William Scrope wrote his 1838 definitive *The Art of Deer Stalking*.

The Glen leading to Minigaig (small) Pass was pounded by drovers and the military, prior to Wade's Drumochter road. From Calvine it continues through the narrowing glen to ascend heather-clad hills and leave Perthshire at the cairned bealach south of Leathad an Taobhain (brae of the rafter), en route for Ruthven Barracks, Kingussie or Glen Feshie. Hamlets, Calvine and Struan (wee burn), head Glen Errochty (assembly) on either side of the River Garry, a spectacular waterway pouring through a gorge of sculptured rock crossed by an incomparable tight knit trio of bridges. A narrow stone, 1760s, road bridge cowers beneath an angled pair of single-track rail bridges of differing generations, one 'up-line' one 'down-line'. Struan Church at Old Struan holds in its burial ground many staunch Jacobites of Clan Donnachaidh (children of Duncan), including the revered Alexander Robertson of Struan who bore arms for Claverhouse, the Earl of Mar and Bonnie Prince Charlie.

Glen Garry ascends to Drumochter (summit ridge) Pass – Perthshire's northern portal below the Sow of Atholl and the Boar of Badenoch, a humourless passage-way that can be snow covered for seventy days a year. It carries major rail and road ways to Inverness, the rail line ascending to 1,484ft (454m) – Britain's highest – and the A9(T) somewhat higher. Both follow Wade's military road (1728–30) that is commemorated on the southern approaches, west of Edendon Bridge. The 'Wade Stone', at layby 70, marks where the working party from Inverness linked with those from Dunkeld.

TO LOCH EARN

From Dunkeld through Strath Braan, the trees thin and surrounding braes dominate at the junction with the A826 leading north to Aberfeldy. Stay with the A822 south to the scattered settlement, the one-time 'Kingshouse' hotel and free-standing church of Amulree at the mouth of Glen Quaich's (cupped hollow) sheeplands. A drover's stance to Crieff and military road prior to entering the Sma' Glen, An Caol Ghleann (the narrow glen), a Victorian acronym bestowed by those wishing to present this pleasing defile as a miniscule Highland glen. In addition to the River Almond,

MILITARY PRECISION

At Aberfeldy (mouth of St Paldoc), Wade's bridge over the Tay is unmistakable, recorded in The House of Commons Journal 1734 *as having 'Starlings of oak and the Piers and land breasts founded on piles shod with iron'. Designed by William Adam, constructed by master masons from Northumbria, it was the closing link of Wade's network of Highland roads. Written on the down-stream parapet is: 'At the command of his majty [sic] King George the 2nd This bridge was erected in the year 1733… committed to the care of Lieut General George Wade Commander in Chief of the forces in Scotland who laid the first stone of this bridge on the 23rd of April and finished the work in the same year'.*

Wade's long-standing military bridge marches over the River Tay at Aberfeldy

Wade's road also passes through, as did Prince Charlie in 1746. There are the remains of a Roman fort and signal station at its southern portal and high on Dun Mor (big fort) a crumbled fort; whilst by river and road a 'giant's grave' and at the north end a striated Clach Ossian (Ossian's stone).

Skirt the Highland Line, with the A822 toward Crieff, passing Glenturret Distillery to join the A85 west to Comrie, once more to plunge into the benign Highlands encircling Loch Lednock Reservoir or St Fillan's and Loch Earn. Glen Lednock's angular dam, together with Breaclaich dam, feeds three power stations and as Lednock fringes the earthquake-sensitive centre around Comrie, its dam was built to resist possible tremors. Watersports and colourful nineteenth-century St Fillan's go hand in hand, as do the surrounding green hills with walks, including the Munro Ben Vorlich (creel-shaped hill) and its partner Stuc a' Chroin (hill of hurt). Grass clad with rocky outcrops, they are accessed from Ardvorlich, west of the burn to Coire Buidhe (yellow corrie), or from Comrie up Glen Artney (Arthur's glen).

RIVER TAY & LOCH TAY

One approach is north on the A826, pioneered by General Wade through upland Glen Cochill. Beyond the dark waters of Loch na Craige stop at the viewpoint/picnic site at GR879464 to absorb Aberfeldy's surrounds, from Glen Lyon's guardians to isolated Schiehallion, then east to coned Farragon Hill and the corral of the Atholl Hills. Other routes leave the A9(T) at Ballinluig to follow the tree-lined Tay, either with the A827 passing the 'one-vehicle' bridge of Grandtully, or north of the river via a scenic minor road passing Strathtay and Cluny Gardens to Weem.

Up-river stands the striking and lightning-struck Black Watch memorial, erected 1887 in appreciation for the freedom of the town. Also restored, Aberfeldy's watermill produces stone-ground oatmeal, fed by the Urlar burn below the Falls of Moness. Visit both, also nearby 'birks (birches) of Aberfeldy', woods that inspired Burns' 'The Birks of Aberfeldie'; and Dewar's World of Whisky, Aberfeldy Distillery, a mecca for devotees of uisgebeatha (water of life).

To Kenmore (big head), through pastured woodland, overlooking the Tay and the floodplain of Appin of Dull (field), passing the small complex stone circle of Croft Moraig (GR798473) and later the policies and pretentious castle of Taymouth, originally Balloch Castle. 'Slippery John', 1st Earl of Breadalbane, arrived to enlarge his seat, which later was, with the Breadalbane dream of endless estates, distended even further. Unfortunately the second Marquis died without issue and so began the estate's decline. A strange tale, but stranger still was the prophecy of the 'Lady of Lawers with the second sight', living in Lawers village. Her prediction, passed on by Gaelic word, revealed the house of Breadalbane would shrivel and waste and that 'The last Campbell would pass over Glenogle leaving nothing behind'. And that is what the 9th Earl did. She also predicted the calamitous 'Breadalbane Clearances' foretelling 'that the teeth of sheep would dislodge the plough'.

Kenmore, at the gates of Taymouth Castle and golf course, shelters beneath Drummond Hill at the east end of Loch Tay. A formal kirk, an old inn of 1760, a fine five-arched brig of 1774 – the first of the Tay's seventeen Perthshire bridges – pleasing cottages, a sailing and walking centre and a well-concealed caravan park make Kenmore a popular holiday destination. Opposite, by the loch's shore, is the Scottish Crannog Centre, a hands-on experience of life in an ancient crannog; and an adjoining, lively watersports centre. The much-loved River Tay (dark), is apparently Scotland's longest river, its initial source, the purists claim, not Loch Tay but the River Canonish springing from Ben Lui.

Loch Tay, Scotland's sixth largest, sweeps west from Kenmore to Killin. Along its tree-clad north shore the regional boundary is met prior to Killin. East of the boundary adjacent to Loch Tay Highland Lodges & Equestrian Centre by Edramucky, a narrow unclassified road ascends north toward Glen Lyon. A scenic roller coaster, that typifies Highland Perthshire, snaking through Lochan na Lairige (loch of the pass) Pass between the Tarmachan (ptarmigan) Ridge and the massif of Ben Lawers, Perthshire's Olympus, a magnet for mountaineers, hill-walkers and due to its unique alpine and arctic flora an attraction for naturalists. Access to the southern

Above: Aberfeldy – lightning struck, the Black Watch memorial looks to Wade's bridge
Below: Kenmore kirk and village at Taymouth below Drummond Hill

Pages 100–1: Tarmachan Ridge and Meall nan Tarmachan – popular with serious trekkers and haven for arctic plants, photographed from summer grazings and long-gone sheilings

side commences from the car park and information centre south of Lochan na Lairige. Other adjoining classics include Creag an Fhithich (cliff of the raven), An Stuc (rocky cone), Lochan nan Cat (cat loch) and Meall Corranaich (hill of the sickle) to the west accessed from the cairned layby (GR594416). Meall nan Tarmachan and Cam Chreag (head of cliff) also nuture arctic plants and provide a serious mountain trek.

GLEN LYON (FLOODING GLEN)

Our next finger of interest is reached from Aberfeldy via Appin of Dull's floodplain, or south from Tummel Bridge to Coshieville. The former passes by Weem (uaimh – cave). General Wade stayed at the inn at Weem whilst his bridge and through road, having been plotted by a survey party of eight with theodolite and chain, were under construction. Restored and mightily impressive Castle Menzies, the 1571 Clan Menzies (pronounced 'Minges') ancestral home a short walk west from Weem, ravaged by Montrose, occupied by Cromwell and stonked by 'Forty-five' Jacobites, is open to seasonal visitors. Glen Lyon, Gleann Dubh nan Garbh Clach (the crooked glen of stones), Scotland's longest and finest enclosed glen, a 33-mile (53km) corridor, in the Pass of Lyon a very narrow corridor, is ringed

Castle Menzies, the sixteenth-century ancestral home of Clan Menzies, now restored

by a near impenetrable mass of remote Grampians. These include Carn Mairg (pudding-shaped hill), Carn Gorm and Meall Buidhe (yellow hill), at its head Beinn a' Chreachain (clam-shell hill), Learg Mheuran (robbers' pass) and Beinn Mhanach (monks' hill); the southern ramparts held firm by Meall Ghaordaidh (hill of wailing) and the Lawers massif.

Fortingall's 200-year-old parish church, and the yew, the latter some 3,000 years older

West from Coshieville, an arborial wonderland contains Europe's oldest living tree and some of the finest beech woods, set in an unequalled mountain glen habitat. Fortingall (churchyard encampment) oozes antiquity, myth and legend. Prehistoric stones and a Middle Ages structure (falsely reputed to be Roman) have been discovered. The word Roman gives rise to a ripper of a tale that credits Fortingall as the birthplace of Pontius Pilate, the fruit of a liaison between a Roman legate and a local lass. An imaginative, traditional Highlands story, unfortunately highly unlikely as the Romans did not arrive until the eighth decade AD.

The simple church, erected in 1900 by Sir Donald Currie, replaced the pre-Reformation church of St Adamnan. Alongside is the Fortingall Yew, at an estimated 3,000 years Europe's oldest living vegetation. Today the taxus is a straggly shadow of the days, 232 years ago, when its trunk's circumference, according to Pennant, was an impressive 56½ft (17.65m). Pleasing nineteenth-century dwellings, not all indigenous, displaying a hint of the Chilterns complete with thatch, grace village and glen. The mountain experience can be enjoyed from Fortingall where paths lead north via Allt Odhar to Gleann Muillin (mill glen), Creag Mhor (big crag) and Carn Mairg, or take the 4½ mile (7.2km) track north, to Glenmore bothy in Gleann Mor beneath Schiehallion.

Entry into hidden Glen Lyon is gained beyond Glen Lyon House, where a wriggling passage threads into the sparsely populated glen via the dramatic Lyon Gorge below Creag Mhor, the site of a clan stramash between landed Campbells and the mainly landless MacGregors, where Gregor MacGregor leapt over the River Lyon to escape his foes. Named 'MacGregor's Leap' this 'long-jump' was attempted again, only once and not in anger, with fatal results. The beech-lined route west passes Chesthill, home of Captain Robert Campbell the reviled perpetrator of the Massacre of Glencoe; and beyond, the ruined Carnbane Castle, home of 'leaping' Gregor MacGregor. Fine views open as the tree curtains thin and the glacial glen floor widens below and between the towering Cairn Mairg and Carn Gorm to the north and Ben Lawers to the south.

Beyond Camusvrachen (speckled bay) two tiny clachans, first Innerwick (shades of the Vikings) with information boards, picnic area and kirk of 1829, and then Bridge of Balgie with combined general store and post office, 11 miles (17.6km) from Glen Lyon's terminus. Here there is a choice of routes, a single-track road to Loch Tay, or westwards through

Upper Glen Lyon: over Loch an Daimh to the coned Creag Doire nan Nathrach

beechwoods past the East Lodge of Maggernie Castle. Originally sixteenth century, this stronghold of 'Mad' Colin Campbell was enlarged in the 1800s and surrounded by beech, lime and conifer. White and in pristine condition when seen from the road, it has an authenticated ghost; visitors are awakened by the warm embrace of a great beauty, whose fine figure ends at her waist. Others report seeing her lower half astride the gravestones in the nearby burial ground, experiences linked to the legend that she was the murdered spouse of a jealous laird.

Electricity came to this remote glen in the 1960s from power stations at the dammed waters of Stronuich (nose) and the enlarged Loch Lyon by Lubreoch (brindled bend) dam. Mixed trees and monocultures are conspicuous by their absence beyond Gallin and the fork right for Loch an Daimh (loch of the stags), apart from a handful of riverside plantations. For those who favour solitude and the mountain scene Glen Lyon is all things, challenging and rewarding. Two such summits are Meall Buidhe coupled with Garbh Meall (rough-water hill) north from Loch an Daimh and the craggy Stuchd an Lochain (peak of the lochs) above Loch an Daimh's southern shore.

LOCHS TUMMEL & RANNOCH

These lie cradled within a 33-mile (53km) east–west glaciated glen over-looked by mighty Schiehallion and a sea of Highland solitude. A journey, from Garry Bridge to Rannoch Station, on the legendary 'Road to the Isles', that inspired the World War I song to include 'By Loch Tummel and Loch Rannoch and Lochaber I will go, by heather tracks wi' heaven in their wiles'. A spectacular winding woodland way, initially above the Linn of Tummel, to the revealing and often busy Queen's View of Loch Tummel (gloomy loch) stretching to the distant guardians of Glen Coe.

Continue west along the wooded north shoreline of Loch Tummel to Tummel Bridge, a small settlement that displays its development for all to see. First came Wade's military road, packhorse bridge and now redundant 'Kingshouse', followed some two centuries later by the Hydroelectric Board, erecting an array of power stations and radiating power-lines. Fortunately Tummel Forest Park's fast growing spruce now mask much of the hydroelectric paraphernalia. The Rev Mitchell penned 'the power stations are an aggressive fea-ture on the landscape. Large areas have been changed in aspect… Beauty spots have been affected and amenities sacri-ficed'. Work began on the Tummel Valley Scheme, led by George Balfour pioneer of hydroelectric, constructing power sta-tions at Rannoch (1930) and Tummel Bridge (1933), followed after the 1939–45 war by stations at Pitlochry, Clunie, Gaur and Errochty. By 1964 nine power sta-tions were 'on stream' fed by tunnels and aqueducts. The 'bridge' of Tummel, built 1733 under the auspices of General Wade, who paid £200 to John Stewart of Kynachan to build it, is a vital link to Trinafour, Drumochter and Inverness. Kingshouse at Tummel Bridge was one of many original billets for Wade's working parties that developed into inns and hostels, called Kingshouses as they stood by the 'King's Highways'.

If Schiehallion has cast its spell take the Tomphubil and Loch Kinardochy road from Tummel Bridge, for on 'The Mound of the Booth' is an interesting limekiln and quarry, and a fine north-west view of the Highland scene. The Schiehallion road runs north-west past the waters of Kinardochy to the Braes of Foss (monument and parking) at Schiehallion's foot: a solitary, quartzite-capped colossus, the cornerstone of the lands of Atholl, Breadalbane and Rannoch, acknowledged as Perthshire's most

A ROYAL RIDDLE

The 'Queen' who originally viewed Loch Tummel is allegedly Isabella, wife of King Robert I who ruled 1306–29, not Victoria who visited in 1866. Proof of Isabella's visit or that she was indeed wife to Robert I, has alluded me. What I have unearthed is that Robert's first wife was Isobel of Mar who died young, his second was Elizabeth de Burgh who died in 1327. No Isabella, although he was crowned at Scone by Isabella, Countess of Buchan; so who was the 'Queen' of the View?

Wade's 1733 Bridge of Tummel, built under contract for £200

The great quartzite hog's-back of Schiehallion rising from the Braes of Foss

charismatic and visible mountain. This 'fairy' hill, and its surrounds, richly endowed with folklore, ghostly legend and eccentricity, has many tales to tell. Stories are recounted in A.D. Cunningham's delightful *Tales of Rannoch*, and by James Robertson writing of his 1870s childhood 'there was no road or path anywhere in the district that was without its ghost'.

Facts concerning Schiehallion are often as strange as fiction, for here in 1774 the Astronomer Royal, Nevil Maskelyne, attempted to determine the mean density of the earth using 'The Attraction of Mountains' theory. His assistant Professor Hutton, whilst assessing the volume of Schiehallion, spawned the 'contour line', that essential cartographic guide for mountaineers. At the conclusion they celebrated with a ceildidh during which fire broke out, gutting the bothy and burning a local lad's fiddle. Replaced by Maskelyne and referred to as the 'Yellow London Lady' it resided in the Clan Donnachaidh Museum at Bruar prior to its closure. On Schiehallion's summit are scattered the ashes of John Duncan Fergusson, the last survivor of the Scottish Colourists. Renowned for his vibrant palette and definite outlines, Fergusson returned from France to found the New Art Club. He died in 1961, requesting his ashes be laid on 'the heart of Scotland' – Schiehallion, later to be joined by those of dancer Margaret Morris.

Recently purchased by the John Muir Trust for £150,000, Schiehallion is noted for its summit limestone pavements and alpine lime-loving flora.

The shortest, and most direct, track to the summit commences at Forest Enterprise car park, east of Braes of Foss farm. Ascend Aonach Ban, then west along the whale-backed ridge for the final cairned kilometre. Be prepared, for underfoot and overhead conditions can change dramatically particularly during the short days of winter. Wise heads avoid the unstable and unpredictable boulders and heathery ways of the northern and southern slopes.

The narrow defile of Strath Fionan (light coloured), with its old homesteads and hut circles, by Dunalastair Water and Innerhadden, leads to Kinloch Rannoch (ferny), conversely sited at the 10-mile (16km) loch's

Above: River Gaur hurrying by Dunan, with Schiehallion's coned summit visible 15 miles (24km) distant

mouth, in spite of its 'Kin' (head) prefix. Note the old bridge over the Tummel, with its interesting albeit double-edged inscription – 'Erected at the sole expense of his Majesty out of the Annexed Estates 1974'. A few centuries ago it was the gate to the Clan MacGregor (children of the mist) bad-lands. Today, the monument to Dugald Buchanan, highly respected Gaelic poet and teacher – 'a teacher of truth and a preacher' – sets the style of Rannoch, as does the loch with its colourful autumnal braes. On its southern shores stands Rannoch School encompassed by Rannoch Forest and Black Wood of Rannoch, a visible and airy remnant of the Caledonian Forest, shrunk due to indiscriminate felling in the 1800s when felled timber was floated, Canadian style, down a series of canals and locks into Loch Rannoch. Black Wood, girdled by moss-covered dykes and carpeted by heaths and heathers, provides parking and a host of forest and fell walks, one legging it through Lairig Ghallabhaich (pass of strange animals) into Glen Lyon.

Below: Rannoch station – our journey's end

From the loch's west end, by Rannoch Barracks and Bridge of Gaur, the road climbs past Gaur power station to Loch Eigheach, a glacial-debris-strewn moonscape loved by the seasonal midge and indigenous deer. Beyond, leave the signposted 'Road to the Isles' for the oasis of Rannoch Station and nearby Loch Laidon (broad loch). Journey's end is on Rannoch Moor, ringed by the bastions of Glen Lyon, with the West Highland Line station, a post office, a cheery tearoom, the Moor of Rannoch Hotel, cottages and a waiting post bus. An exit, world's away from our Forth Bridge's entrance, that provides the perfect portal through which to reluctantly take our leave of Fife, Perthshire and Kinross. *Soraidh le Rannoch* – Farewell to Rannoch.

Useful Information & Places to Visit

MAPS

Ordnance Survey:
Landranger 1:50 000,
41 Ben Nevis & surrounding area, 42 Glen Garry & Loch Rannoch area, 43 Braemar & Blair Atholl, 51 Loch Tay & surrounding area, 52 Pitlochry to Crieff, 53 Blairgowrie, 58 Perth & Alloa, Auchterader, 59 St Andrews, Kirkcaldy and Glenrothes, 65 Falkirk & Linlithgow, Dunfermline, 66 Edinburgh & North Berwick Outdoor Leisure 38, 1:25 000, Ben Nevis and Glen Coe

Harveys:
Superwalker, 1:25 000, Ochil Hills

LOCAL NEWSPAPERS

Fife: *Central Fife Times & Advertiser, Dunfermline Press & West of Fife Advertiser, Dunfermline Herald & Post* (free), *East Fife Mail, Evening Telegraph & Post, Fife Free Press, Fife Herald, Fife & Kinross Extra, Fife Leader* (free), *Glenrothes Gazette, St Andrews Citizen*

Perth & Kinross: *Blairgowrie Advertiser, Evening Telegraph & Post, Perth Shopper* (free), *Perthshire Advertiser, Strathearn Herald*

TOURIST INFORMATION CENTRES

General information, accommodation from hotels to campsites and a book-a-bed service, fishing permits and theatre tickets.

Fife

Anstruther (Apr–Sept): Scottish Fisheries Museum, Harbourhead, Anstruther KY10 3BA
Tel: 01333 311073

Crail (Apr–Sept): Crail Museum & Heritage Centre, 62–64 Marketgate, Crail KY10 3TL
Tel: 01333 450869

Dunfermline (Apr–Sept): 13/15 Maygate, Dunfermline KY12 7NE
Tel: 01383 720999
Fax: 01383 625807

Forth Bridges: c/o Queensferry Lodge Hotel, North Queensferry KY11 1HP
Tel: 01383 417759

Kirkcaldy (Apr–Sept): 19 Whitecauseway, Kirkcaldy KY1 1XF
Tel: 01592 267775
Fax: 01592 203154

St Andrews: 70 Market Street, St Andrews KY16 9NU
Tel: 01334 472021
Fax: 01334 478422

Perth & Kinross
Aberfeldy: The Square, Aberfeldy PH15 2DD
Tel: 01887 820276
Fax: 01887 829495

Auchterader: 90 High Street, Auchterader PH3 1BJ
Tel: 01764 663450
Fax: 01764 664235

Blairgowrie: 26 Wellmeadow, Blairgowrie PH10 6AS
Tel: 01250 872960
Fax: 01250 873701
Ski-Line: 01250 875800

Crieff: High Street, Crieff PH7 3HU
Tel: 01764 652578
Fax: 01764 655422

Dunkeld: The Cross, Dunkeld PH8 0AN
Tel: 01350 727688
Fax: 01350 727688

Kinross: Service Area, Junction 6 (M90), Kinross KY13 7NQ
Tel: 01577 863680
Fax: 01577 863370

Perth: Lower City Mills, West Mill Street, Perth PH1 5QP
Tel: 01738 450600
Fax: 01738 444863

Perth: Caithness Glass, Inveralmond, Perth PH1 3TZ
Tel: 01738 638481

Pitlochry: 22 Atholl Road, Pitlochry PH16 5BX
Tel: 01796 472215/472751
Fax: 01796 474046

A comprehensive list of history & heritage, museums & collections, parks & gardens, visitor centres & crafts, specialist outdoor/indoor activities, shops, places to eat etc is included in the annual *Essential Guide to Fife, Explore Perthshire* and *Where to Stay – Fife & Perthshire,* available from Tourist Information Centres.

GETTING ABOUT

Train: National Rail Enquiry 0345 484950
ScotRail Telesales 0345 550033
Fife: Edinburgh to Aberdeen service stops at six stations, and the Fife Circle trains call at fourteen stations; timetables available at all stations and Tourist Information Centres
Perth: Links from Edinburgh and Glasgow call at five stations, including Pitlochry and Blair Atholl on the Highland Line and Rannoch on the West Highland Line; timetables from all stations and Tourist Information Centres
Coach/bus: National Express and Citylink coaches link Fife, Perth and Kinross with the majority of major towns and cities throughout Britain
Timetables/reservations:
Citylink 0990 505050
National Express 0990 808080
Local bus services & post bus: information from Tourist Information Centres and bus stations. The post bus connects with Rannoch Station
Fife Council's Public Transport Information Line: 01592 416060;
Perth & Kinross Council's Public Transport Information: 0845 3011130

Air: Edinburgh Airport – 30 minutes from Fife and Perth
Glasgow Airport – 75 minutes from Fife and Perth

YOUTH HOSTELS

Glendevon, Kinross: 01259 781206
Perth: 01738 623658
Pitlochry: 01796 472308

MOUNTAIN SEARCH AND RESCUE

Tel: Freephone 999
(Police – to alert and co-ordinate rescue services)

WEATHER FORECASTS

Scottish Meteorological Services: Glasgow Weather Centre 0141 2483451
WeatherCall 7 Day 0891 505351
MarineCall 5 Day 0891 505351
Ski reports & avalanche update – Ski-Line 01250 875800
Television & radio:
   BBC1 Scotland 5-day forecast, 18.55hrs Mon–Fri
   Hillwalking, skiing and sailing forecast 18.55hr Fri BBC1 & BBC2 and Ceefax 402
ITV Scotland Channel 3: daily forecasts, Mon–Fri Teletext 105
BBC Radio Scotland FM: daily forecast, hillwalker's forecast Fri 19.30hr Sat/Sun 07.03hr

DEER STALKING

From August to October recorded telephone messages will provide information on the location of deer-stalking activities in Perthshire's Highlands.

Drumochter: 01528 522200
Glen Shee: 01250 885288
Rannoch Moor: 01882 633248
For Loch Rannoch, Glen Lyon, Loch Tay and Strathearn enquire from the local tourist office.

MISCELLANEOUS ADDRESSES

Historic Scotland, 20 Brandon Place, Edinburgh EH3 5RA

Scottish Natural Heritage, 16 Hope Terrace, Edinburgh EH12 9DQ

Scottish Rights of Way Society, John Cotton Business Centre, 10/12 Sunnyside, Edinburgh EH17 5RA

Scottish Youth Hostels Association, 7 Glebe Crescent, Stirling FK8 2JA
Tel: 01786 891400

The Mountaineering Council of Scotland, 4a St Catherines Road, Perth PH1 5SE
Tel: 01738 638227

The National Trust for Scotland, 28 Charlotte Square, Edinburgh EH2 4ET

BIBLIOGRAPHY

Baker, E. A. O*n Foot in the Highlands* (Alexander Maclehose, 1932)

Ballingall, William. *The Shores of Fife* (Edmonston and Douglas: Edinburgh 1872, reprint 1995)

Bennet, Donald. *The Southern Highlands* (The Scottish Mountaineering Trust, 1972)

Brown, Hamish. *The Fife Coast* (Mainstream, 1994)

Bruce, William Scott. *The Railways of Fife* (Melven Press, Perth 1980)

Caledonian Road School. *Bridges of the Tay* (Perth and Kinross District Library Service, 1982)

Campbell, Margaret. *Strange Tales of Perthshire* (Lang Syne Publishers, 1990)

Campbell, Steven. *Enjoying Perthshire* (Perth & Kinross District Libraries, 1994)

Duncan, Jeremy. *Perth and Kinross – The Big Country* (John Donald Publishers Ltd, 1991)

Drummond, Peter. *Scottish Hill and Mountain Names* (Scottish Mountaineering Trust, 1991)

Gordon, Seton. *Highways and Byeways in the Central Highlands* (Birlinn Ltd, Edinburgh 1995)

Geddie, John. *The Fringes of Fife* (W. & R. Chambers Limited, 1894)

Gordon, T. Crouther. *Beautiful Pitlochry* (L. Mackay, 1955)

Graham Campbell, David. *Perth – The Fair City* (J. Donald, 1992)

Haldane, A.R.B. *The Drove Roads of Scotland* (T. Nelson & Sons Ltd, 1952)

Keay, John & Julia. *Collins Encyclopaedia of Scotland* (Harper Collins, 1994)

Lang, Andrew. *James VI and the Gowrie Mystery* (Longmans, Green, 1902)

Lamont-Brown, Raymond. *Discovering Fife* (John Donald Publishers Ltd, 1988)

Mackerracher, A. C. *Perthshire in History and Legend* (John Donald Publishers Ltd, 1988)

McGonagall, William. *Poetic Gems* (David Winter & Son Ltd, Dundee. Gerald Duckworth & Co Ltd, London 1963)

Morton, H. V. *In Search of Scotland* (Methuen London Ltd, 1929, paperback 1984)

Murray, Howard J. *A King's Treasure Lost* (Silver Screens Print plc [Scottish Division] 1999)

Ogilvy, Graham. *Fife and its People* (Mainstream Publishing Co, 1996)

Omand, Donald (ed). *The Perthshire Book* (Birlinn, 1997)

Roger, Charles. *History of St Andrews* (Adam & Charles Black, Edinburgh 1849)

Sinclair, Sir John (ed). *Statistical Account of Scotland 1791–1799 – Vol X Fife* (EP Publishing Ltd, 1978)

Sinclair, Sir John (ed). *Statistical Account of Scotland 1791–1799 – Vol XI South and East Perthshire, Kinross-shire* (EP Publishing Ltd, 1976)

Smith, Peter. *History of Steam and the East Fife Fishing Fleet* (James Corstorphine, Leven 1998)

Smith, Roger. *Highland Perthshire* (HMSO, 1994)

Stavert, Marion L. *Perth – A Short History* (Perth and Kinross District Libraries, 1991)

Taylor, David B. (ed). The Third Statistical Account of Scotland. *The Counties of Perth and Kinross* (Culross the Printers, Coupar Angus 1979)

Walker, Bruce, and Ritchie, Graham. *Exploring Scotland's Heritage, Fife and Tayside* (HMSO, 1987)

ACKNOWLEDGEMENTS

In spite of the constantly changing landscape, architecture, economic and social history, industry and climate throughout the considerable acreage of Fife and Perthshire, including Kinross, there remained one unchangeable factor: those who, when asked by a complete stranger, willingly gave of their help, time and knowledge. My appreciative thanks to the staff of Dunfermline Library and Perth's A.K. Bell Library, Fife Tourist Board and Perthshire Tourist Board, Pitlochry Youth Hostel and Eilean Eaton, of the Meigle Museum.

For Gaelic guidance to a Sassenach my thanks to Jennifer Marshall of Inveroran and Calum Smith of Fort William. Closer to home the always available grammatic and photographic guidance of Greta and Hector and on behalf of my temperamental, much-maligned computer, the invaluable curative skills of Kevin.

INDEX

Page numbers in *italic* indicate illustrations

Aberdour, *25*; Robert the Bruce, 25; Hawkcraig Jetty, *10*, 25; Inchcolm, 25–6

Aberfeldy: Birks of, 98; Black Watch Memorial, 98, *99*; Wade's military bridge, *98*, 98

Abernethy, *73*; biscuit, 73; Celtic round tower, 73; Pictish capital, 73

airports, 11; RAF Station, Leuchars, 45

airfields: Fife Airport, Glenrothes, 12; Scone Aerodrome, Perth; 12 Scottish Gliding Centre, Levenmouth, Fife, 12, 67

Alyth, 85, *86*; folk museum, 85

Anstruther: Paul Jones, 39; *QE2*, 36; Scottish Fisheries Museum, 36

arctic flora, 99, 102, 106

Atholl: Blair, 95; castle, 95; Dukes, 90, 92; lands, 105

Auchterarder: Creed, 76; Jacobites, 76; Test Case, 76

Auchtermuchty, 51; Sir Jimmy Shand, 51

Balbirnie Country Park, 58; House, *58*

Balmerino Abbey, 48

Benarty Hill, 65

Ben y Vrackie, 94, *95*

Blairgowrie & Rattray: Donald Cargill, *85*, 86; mills (restored), 85; raspberries, *86*, 86

Bishop Hill, *60-1*, 60

Braan: river, 92; Strath 96

Bridges: Forth rail, 10, *16-17*, 17; Forth road, *7*; Tay rail, 10, *47*; Tay road, *47*

Bridge of Earn: gateway, 73; carbonated spring water, 74; Rennie's Bridge, 74

Bruar: Falls, 95, 96; Lodge, 96; museum, 95, 106; water – Robert Burns, 96

Buchanan, Dugald, 107

Burntisland, 26; Royal Gold,

26; St Columba's, 26; train–transporter ferry, 26

Cairnwell, The: *83*, 83; Devil's Elbow, 88; Glenshee Ski Centre, 88; Pass, 88, *88-9*

Canmore, House of, 9; Malcolm III, 23, 76; Robert I the Bruce, 23, 25

Carnegie, Andrew, 11; benefactions, 11, 23; birthplace, 23, 24

Carse of Gowrie, 62, *72-3*, 82; brickworks, 82; Errol, 82; Rait, 82; reed beds, 82

Castle Menzies, *102*, 102

Ceres: Bishop Bridge, *53*; June Games, 53; Magus Muir, 53; provost, *53*

Charlestown, 18

Claverhouse: John Graham, 85, 95

Cleish Hills, including Dumglow & Knockhill (Racing Circuit), 22

coal mining: Buckhaven, 30; Coaltown of Wemyss, *29*, 29; Culross, 18, 19; Kirkcaldy, 27; Lochgelly, 24, 29; Lochore, 24; Markinch, 58

coal ports: Kirkcaldy, 26; Methil, 30; West Wemyss, *28*, 29

Comrie, *77*; Earthquake House, 77; Rennie Bridge, 77

Crail, 36; capon, 38; fishing, 38; harbour, *13*, 38; John Knox, 38, 39; St Mary's, 38, *39*

Crieff, *79*; Jacobites, 78; railway, 78; Tryst, 78

Crombie, burial ground, 18

Cromwell, 26, 55, 80, 87, 95, 102

Culross, 18, 19; Sir George Bruce, 18, 19; chalder, 19; palace, *1*, 19; restoration, 18, 19; Rev Roland, 19; salt, 19; town house, *18*

Cupar, *51*, *52*, 51, 52

deer: William Scrope, 96; stalking, 96

Defoe, Daniel, 34; Leslie House, 57; *Robinson Crusoe*, 11, *34*, 34

drovers, 68, 78, 87

Drummond Castle Gardens, *76*, 77

Drumochter: Pass, 96; railway, 96; Wade's stone, 96

Dundas Henry, 1st Viscount Melville, 77

Dunkeld: cathedral, 90, 92, *93*; bridge, 92; Neil Gow, 92; plumbing, 92

Dunfermline: abbey, *23*, 24; Athletic FC – Jock Stein, 24; Carnegie Museum, 13, 24; linen weaving, 23; Pittencrieff Park, *22*, 23, 24; wildlife, 23

Dunning, 74, *75*; 'fee-ing', 74; Jacobites, 75; Romans, 75; St Serf's, 74, *75*

Dysart, 28; crow-stepped skews, 28; St Serf's, 28; salt and nails, 28; smugglers, 28

Earlsferry, 34; James Braid, 34; MacDuff, Earl of 'Fyfe', 34

Edradour, distillery, 94

Elie, 34, 35; Lady's Tower, *35*, 35; railway station, 35

Falkland: House of Stewart, 55; palace, *55*, 55; Pictish stones, 55

Fergusson: John Duncan, 106

Fife Ness: air station, 38, 39; North Carr Beacon, 38

fishing: Anstruther, 32, 36; Buckhaven, 30; Crail, 38; Earlsferry & Elie, 34; Fife's East Neuk, *32*; Kilrenny, 36; Loch Leven, 66; Loch Moraig, 95; Newburgh, 50; Pittenweem, *36*, 36; St Monance, 35; Tay, 62; Tentsmuir, 45

Forgandenny: powered

flight, 74; Strathallen School, 74

Forth: Firth of, 7, 15; ferry, 17, 26, 34; railway company, 17

Fortingall: church and yew, *103*; Pontius Pilot, 11, 103

Garry Bridge, 94

geology, 8, 68, 83

Glen Almond: Romans, 78; Trinity College, 78; weaving/bleaching, 78

Glen Eagles, 69, *70-1*

Glen Garry, 96

Glen Lyon, 102–4; Captain Robert Campbell, 103; ghosts, 104; hydro-electric, 104; MacGregor's Leap, *9*, 103; mountains/lochs, 103, *104*

Glen Shee: Devil's Elbow, *88-9*; Major Caulfeild, 87; ski centre *83*, 83; Spital of, 87

Glen Tilt, 95

Gleneagles Hotel & Golf Course, *76*, 76, 77

Glenrothes: 57; sculptures, *57*

golf: Balbirnie, 58; Balcomie, 38; Crieff, 78; Gleneagles, 77; Ladybank, 54; Lundin Links, *32*; Pitlochry, 94; Rosemount, 86; St Andrews, 40, *43*, 43, 44; Strathearn, 77

Guardbridge, 44; Archbishop Beaton, 44

Hermitage/Ossian's Hall, *92*, 92

hydro-electric, 7, 104, 105, 107

Inverkeithing: Hospitium, 18; Lammas Fair, 17, 18; mercat cross, *18*, 18

Isle of May: lighthouse, 38; St Adrian, 38; shipping toll, 38

Jacob, Violet, 7

John Muir Trust, 106

Johnson, Dr Samuel/Boswell, James, 11, 26, 43, 44, 90
jougs, 53, 66, 90

Kenmore, *99*, 99; crannog, 99
Killiecrankie: Battle, 95; Pass, 94, 95, *97*; Jacobite soldier's leap, 95
Kincardine, 19, 22
Kinghorn, Royal mint, 26
Kinloch Rannoch, 107
Kinnesswood: Michael Bruce, Alexander Buchan, 57
Kinnoull Hill, *72–3*, 81–2
Kilrenny: church, 36; doocotes, 36, *38*
Kinross, 8; Bruce mausoleum, *66*, 67; cashmere, 76; house, 66
Kirkcaldy, 13, 26, 27; linoleum, 27; Ravenscraig Castle, *4, 5, 27, 27,* 28; A. Smith, 7
Kirkmichael: drovers, 87; Jacobites, 87
Knox, John, 11, 43, 80

Lawers: Ben, *2, 3,* 99; Lady of, 98
Largo: Law, 34, *35*; Lower, *32–3,* 34; Alexander Selkirk, 11, 34, *34*; Upper, 32, 34
Lee, Jennie MP, 24
Leslie: bull stone, *57*; Earls of Rothes, 50
Leuchars: RFC & RAF, 44; St Athernase, 44, *45*
Leven: golf links, 30; Letham Glen, 30; smuggling, 30
Limekilns, 18, *19*; R. L. Stevenson, 18
Lochs: an Daimh, *104*; Butterstone, 92, *93*; Earn, 96; Faskally, *12*, 94; Glow, 22; Leven: 8, 11,*64–5, 65,* 65, 66; of the Lowes, 92; Lyon, 104; Moraig, 95; Ordie, 92; Rannoch, 107; Tay; *62-3*; Tummel: *105,* 105
Lochore Meadows Country Park, *24,* 24

Logierait, 94
Lomond Hills, *15*,15, *59,* 56–60; rock climbs, 60; wildlife, 59
Longannet power station and coal mine, 19, *20–1*
Lundin Links stone circle, *32,* 32

Mac-Alpin, Kenneth, 8
McGonagall, William, 10, 45, 66, 88
Maggernie Castle, ghosts, 104
Markinch: Country Park, 50; Picts – Balfarg & Balbirnie, 50
Mary, Queen 'of Scots', 11, 66
Meigle Pictish Museum, 85
Meikleour hedge, *85,* 85
Methil: 30; coal port, 29, 30; oil rigs, *30–1*, 30; 'Slim' Jim Baxter, 30
Mossmorran chemical complex, *24,* 24
Moulin: Ben-y-Vrackie, 94, *95*; hotel, *94,* 94; kirk and burial ground, 94

Newburgh, *48–9*; Lindores Abbey, 50; museum, 51; port, *50,* 51
Newport on Tay, 45, *47,* 47; ferry, 45
North Queensferry, 17; Deep Sea World Aquarium, 17

Ochil Hills, 68, 69

Perth: bull sales, 81; museums, 13, 80; North Inch, 80; Old Waterworks, *80,* 80; St John's, 80; Sir Walter Scott, 80; Smeaton's Bridge, 80–1, *81*
Pettycur, 26; ferry, 26; Inchkeith, 26; trans-Fife coaches, 26, 45, 54
Picts, 8; Abernethy, 73; Dunfa landy, 94; Falkland, 55; Meigle, *84,* 85; Perth, 80; Scone, 82; silverware,

34; symbolic stones, 8, *84*;
Pitlessie (David Wilkie), 54
Pitlochry: festival theatre, 94; hydro-electric centre, *8,* 94; Queen Victoria, 94; sculptures, *94,* 94
Pittenweem: Covenanters, 36; Porteous riots, 36

Queen's View, *105,* 105

railways, 11; Drumochter, 96; Elie, 34, 35; Cupar, 52; Ladybank, 54; Largo, 34; rail ferry, 26, 45; West Highland Line, 107
Rannoch: Black Wood, 107; moor, *101*; station, *107,* 107
roads, 11; to the Isles, 94, 95, 105, *107*
Romans, 8
Rosyth, 18, *19*
Ruthven Castle (Huntingtower), *78*; Ruthven Raid and Thomas Pennant, 78
Rumbling Bridge: flora, *68,* 68

St Andrews: Archbishop Beaton and Cardinal Beaton, 43; castle, *42,* 43; cathedral, *40,* 42; *Chariots of Fire,* 11; golf, 11, *43,* 43, 44; kite-ing, 11, *40–1*; martyrs, 43; museum, 13, 44; Reformation, 43; Royal & Ancient, 43, 44; St Andrew, 42; St Regulus (Rule), 42, *43*; university, 40, 43; William Wallace, 42
St Monans, 35; church, 35; Newark Castle, 35; salt, 35, *37*
Saline, 22; God's Acre's headstones, 22
Schiehallion, *90–1, 105, 106,* 105; Prof Hutton, Neil Maskelyne, 106
Scone, 82, *82*
Scotstarvit Tower, *54,* 54
Scott, Sir Walter, 15, 80, 84
Sma' Glen, 96, 98
Smith, Mary C., 13

Stanley: Bell Mill, *84,* 84
Stewart, House of, 9, 23, 55; Mary Queen 'of Scots', 66; James IV, 55
Strathardle, 86–7
Strathearn, *72-3, 74,* 73
Strathmiglo: Picts, 56; public right of way, 56; tolbooth, *14*
Strathmore, *83, 83,* 85; raspberries, *83,* 86
Struan: church – Jacobites, 96; triple bridge, *96,* 96

Tarmachan Ridge, 99, *100–1*
Tay: river, 45, 47, *47,* 98, 99; loch, 62; 98, 99; salmon, 50, 51
Taymouth Castle: Earl of Breadalbane, 98; Lady of Lawers, 98, 99
Tayport, 45, *46*
Tentsmuir: nature reserve, 44, 45; salmon fishers, 45
Tummel, bridge, *105,* 105

Wade, General George: bridges and roads, 8, 87, 90, 94, 96, *98,* 98, 105
walks: Blairgowrie, 86; Ben Vorlich, 98; Cateran Way, 87; Dunkeld, 92; Fife Coastal Path, 17, 34; Fortingall, 103; Glen Lyon, 103–4; Lomond Hills, *56,* 56, 58–60; Minigaig Pass, 96; Pitlochry Autumn Festival, *12,* 94; St Andrews, 43
Wemyss: Coaltown of, *29,* 29; East, 30; West, *28,* 29
witches: Anstruther, 38; Crook o' Devon, 68; Dunning, 75; Forgandenny, 74; Inverkeithing, 18; Pittenweem, 36; Newburgh, 51

Yetts o' Muckhart: toll road, 68